DIPA KARMAKAR

THE SMALL WONDER

Bishweshwar Nandi | Digvijay Singh Deo | Vimal Mohan

FINGERPRINT!

Published by
FINGERPRINT!
An imprint of Prakash Books India Pvt. Ltd.

113/A, Darya Ganj,
New Delhi-110 002
Tel: (011) 2324 7062 – 65, Fax: (011) 2324 6975
Email: info@prakashbooks.com/sales@prakashbooks.com

facebook www.facebook.com/fingerprintpublishing
twitter www.twitter.com/FingerprintP
www.fingerprintpublishing.com

Photo credits:
Page 45: Courtesy-Mrs Sushila Devi
Page 49, 51: Courtesy-Bharat Kishore Deb Burma
Page 55: Courtesy-Coach Mantu Debnath
Page 57 bottom to 63 : Courtesy-Seshadri Sukumar
Page 92, 94, 101: Courtesy-BS Nandi
Page 49, 103, 106 to 108, 145, 146 bottom, 147 bottom, 148 to 152:
Courtesy-Metro Media Works

ISBN: 978 93 8836 950 3

Processed & printed in India

This book is dedicated to
my coach Bishweshwar Nandi without
whom this 'four-foot something' gymnast
would not have achieved anything that
has been possible over the last
decade and a half.

CONTENTS

FOREWORD

Hello, India. I hope you are extremely proud of Dipa Karmakar.

You do not need to be born in a particular country to be good at gymnastics. Yes, over the years USA, Russia, and Romania have dominated the sport but it is fascinating to see a talented gymnast like Dipa emerge from India. Her success will ensure that it is no longer considered a bridge too far for an Indian to shine at the world stage in the extremely competitive sport of gymnastics.

It is not important for everyone to become a Dipa but it is extremely important that we have role models to inspire children to play sport. India is known the world over as a country very passionate about cricket but the last decade has seen many other champions from other sports emerge and it is very heartening to see gymnastics enter the mind-space, thanks to the performances of Dipa at international events and especially the Rio Olympic Games.

I was there in Rio for the 2016 Olympics and was very surprised to see Dipa attempt the Produnova. It is an extremely difficult and complex vault, yet she executed it with minimum fuss. As someone who has competed at the highest level, I must say that it requires a lot of guts and had I been given a choice, I would never have attempted such a dangerous vault. It is truly a reflection of the bravery and the dedication of this lovely gymnast that she was successful in executing it at a place no less than the Olympics. Decades from now they will still be watching it on YouTube.

I was just fourteen and a half years old when I competed at my first Olympics in Montreal in 1976. I was aware that the Olympics were a big competition but a true understanding of what the Olympics actually meant came much later, at the Moscow Olympics in 1980. Winning at the Olympics is the biggest achievement for a sportsperson and I was fortunate to enjoy that winning feeling at both Montreal and Moscow.

Perhaps it is my destiny that I will forever be remembered as the first gymnast to score a perfect ten at the Olympics. To be honest, I think one of the reasons I became an international celebrity at the Montreal Games was due to the circumstances of that 10. The scoreboard was not configured to display a 10 and I remember the gasp around the arena when the scoreboard displayed a 1.00 after my routine on the uneven bars. Of course at that time I never realised why it was such a huge thing but even today, forty-two years later, it is still the most talked about performance in our sport. It resonated with an entire generation and that is also the connect with Dipa.

Dipa's performances have clearly struck a chord with the people of India. She may not have had the access to the facilities we enjoyed or the best gymnasts of the world have today but she has a passion for her sport. To succeed in sport you need to have passion. It is this which will see you negotiate the hurdles that you face over your career.

Dipa came agonisingly close to a medal at Rio, but there is no need for her to change anything ahead of Tokyo. You have to strive to be the best you can be everyday. She does not need to move overseas to be able to challenge for a medal at the next Olympics. She clearly has a very supportive system in India and all I would suggest to her is to perhaps go abroad and train, either in America or any other country where there are good gymnasts, for just a short while. Just a week or two to change the environment and then back to India.

Hopefully she achieves her dream at Tokyo and hopefully she has already made an entire generation of children fall in love with our beautiful sport.

Nadia Comăneci
FIVE-TIME OLYMPIC CHAMPION AND MEMBER,
LAUREUS WORLD SPORTS ACADEMY

AUTHORS' NOTES

Bishweshwar Nandi

Dipa Karmakar's rise in Indian sport caught most of India unawares. "Oh, she is the gymnast who does the death vault," is what we usually got to hear. I would get really upset as the very mention of the word 'death' was something I avoided bringing up in front of Dipa. One can practice as much as possible, but one cannot control the mind. One misstep in gymnastics, and especially the Produnova vault, can lead to disaster and the end of a career.

There is a lot more to Dipa than the Produnova. I have been training her since she was ten years old. That mischievous brat who never listened to me has today ensured that I am mentioned alongside her whenever the conversation turns to gymnastics. To be honest, her story is my story. Together we have battled the odds and endured a lot of humiliation and ridicule along the way.

This book is an attempt to share our story with a wider audience. Dipa was inundated with questions post her fourth place finish at the Rio Olympics. An entire generation seemed oblivious to the history of gymnastics in Tripura and we were supposed to have emerged from nowhere. There was an urgent need to change the narrative, about our state and our gymnastics.

I am grateful to Vimal Mohan and Digvijay Singh Deo for convincing both Dipa and me to share our story through them. I must admit we were rather anxious as we were not fully aware of the effort needed for a book on Dipa's life and career. Our focus had turned to the 2020 Tokyo Olympics the moment we flew out of Rio and I did not want any distractions. Viimal and Digvijay convinced me over multiple sittings that Dipa's practice would not be affected one bit and that our story had to be told to inspire a new generation. Over the course of this book, they have travelled to Tripura, met gymnasts who once ruled the Indian gymnastics scene, and have returned educated about the contribution of our state to the sport of gymnastics. Both Dipa and I have been honest and it is not our intention to settle scores or create controversy. There are many Dipas out there who have not received the right opportunity to break through but I am confident they will be inspired by Dipa's story and chart their own course to success.

Bishweshwar Nandi

Digvijay Singh Deo

I must confess I did not see Dipa Karmakar's historic vault at the Rio Olympics. Such is the nature of a multi-discipline event that you cannot be at two places at once. It had been a very poor Olympics for India till the 14th of August 2016 and we journalists were clutching at straws. Any chance of a medal meant you had to be there.

I still remember the discussion with my the then colleague Vimal Kumar, the sports editor of IBN7 or News18 India as it was rebranded just ahead of the Olympics. For the sake of convenience we had booked a flat not too far away from the media centre of the Rio Olympics. Past experience of having been at the Olympics meant mobility was essential and the media centre had round-the-clock shuttle services to all the Olympic venues. Vimal and I were sharing resources, with us having just one video journalist, Pradeep Kumar Das, for the nearly month-long trip to Rio de Janeiro.

The first week of the Olympics had been one of near misses. The 2008 Olympic Champion Abhinav Bindra retired from shooting by finishing an agonising fourth in his 10 metre air rifle event. Jitu Rai reached the final of the 10 metre air pistol event on the first day of the Olympics but the rest of the contingent had not been able to break India's duck at the Games.

Tennis was a sport where India had a strong chance but Leander Paes and Rohan Bopanna lost in the first round of the men's doubles and the same evening Sania Mirza and Prarthana Thombare crashed out of the women's doubles. The only good thing that came out that evening was the chance to watch the match with Bharat Ratna Sachin Tendulkar sitting ten feet away.

Mirza and Bopanna raised hopes of a medal for India by reaching the semi-final of the mixed doubles event. They had notched up some pretty impressive wins including one over Sir Andy Murray and Heather Watson in the quarter final. A silver medal looked assured when Mirza and Bopanna, playing flawless tennis, took the first set against Venus Williams and Rajeev Ram in the semis. Williams, though, is a champion of the highest calibre and she turned the match around singlehandedly in the second set and then inspired Ram as well to beat the Indian pair in the deciding match tie-break.

A medal had once again eluded us and the morale was pretty low among us in the press corps. Mirza and Bopanna were then scheduled to play the bronze medal match the next morning against the pairing of Radek Stepanek and Lucie Hradecka. That threw our schedule completely off track. Within minutes of the match kicking off, India were to take on Belgium in the quarter-finals of the men's hockey competition at the Olympic hockey centre in Deodoro. It was the first time India had reached the knockout round at an Olympics in hockey since 1980 and considering India's past record it was imperative that we were there at that game as well. Later that afternoon Dipa was scheduled to compete in the final of the women's vault.

After much debate it was decided that I would head off to the tennis centre which was not too far away while Vimal would go to cover the hockey match which was at a considerable distance from the Olympic park. It turned out to be a disappointing outing for both of us; Mirza and Bopanna could not recover from the setback of the previous evening and looked emotionally drained as they lost in straight sets. Over in Deodoro, the Indian hockey team too saw its campaign end after a 1-3 reversal against Belgium.

I was pretty upset, understandably so, having covered the length and breadth of India from February 2016 till the end of June 2016, shooting a six-episode news documentary titled 'India's Champions' for CNN-News18. We had spent days covering various teams preparing for the Olympics, sharing a meal with them, and shooting them in a setting where they went about their training while we hung around in the background, capturing every small titbit on tape.

I was asked by my team back in New Delhi to be available for a live update just after the tennis campaign ended. It was a one-hour broadcast and the mood was pretty sombre with the two results knocking the wind out of our sails.

Dipa's event was about to get underway and as I sat down for the live broadcast, Vimal returned from the hockey match. I asked him to immediately head over to the gymnastics venue while I analysed the disappointing trend on CNN-News18. Vimal just about managed to get to the venue in time; it was ten minutes away from the media centre and I was happy we had someone there. I followed the minute-by-minute update on the live results section on my iPad and tweets of fellow reporters there. Dipa did not win a medal, but she won hearts with a performance that had no parallel in Indian sport.

Later that evening I read a piece by Gaurav Kalra, a dear friend and my former sports editor on ESPN.in, where he wrote about being reduced to tears by Dipa's performance. Reading it, I started kicking myself at having missed a historic moment in Indian sport. However, when you cover the Olympics you have to be mentally at peace with not being at all the right places at particular moments.

That night, my friend Vimal Mohan, who covers sports for NDTV India and who knew Bishweshwar Nandi pretty well, convinced both Nandi and Karmakar to meet the electronic media outside the Games Village. Mohan has been a trendsetter in TV journalism; he has dedicated his career to covering 'other sports', as he says. He is always there at domestic meets, at IOA meetings, and on a personal note I have always looked up to him as a driving force in my career. Mohan has been the benchmark for a generation of us sports reporters and I am grateful that despite our occasional tiffs and fallouts, we have stuck together, bound by our love for sport.

There was something about Dipa's journey that fascinated me. I too was eager to know where did this champion emerge from as I too had been guilty of thinking of Tripura as just another state that had lucked out due to a once-in-a-lifetime sportsperson. There were a couple of interactions with Nandi and Karmakar in Rio and I could sense they were upset with the stuff being written about them and their journey. By this time I had received a call from my agent Kanishka Gupta suggesting that India needed to know the story of Dipa Karmakar and I turned to Mohan to broach the topic with Karmakar and Nandi. Convincing them was entirely his domain but they warmed up to the idea as they had been swept away by an outpouring of euphoria on their return to India. Nandi was categorical that Dipa's practice and training was non-negotiable and made it clear that time was not something he could promise. The rules of the game were clear but Mohan and I decided to go along for the ride. We are journalists after all, and every story presents a new opportunity to learn.

We did not account for a couple of things. A few days before our first trip to Tripura to meet Dipa and her family, the Indian government announced the demonetisation drive. It left us in a peculiar situation where we had flight tickets and accommodation booked but no money in our wallets. Once again Mohan bailed us out, delving into his deep network of friends to get us to a bank (will not mention which one or where, for obvious reasons) where we managed to exchange our old, worthless notes for legal tender.

The trip to Agartala was an eye-opener; it was not an outpost of Indian sport as we had imagined but a full-fledged system that had churned out an assembly line of champions in gymnastics over the years. Every facet, every detail, every nugget was noted down and as we began to piece this remarkable story together, our prejudices too got broken down.

Dipa Karmakar has shown that you do not need the best of equipment, the exposure that our sportspersons regularly demand, to succeed at the highest level. What you need is determination and a will to win and then things will fall your way. The will to win is extremely important; she is an example to millions of Indians that they too can pursue their dreams. I could not pursue my dream of playing sport at the top level, dissuaded by a nascent sports scene in Odisha, where I grew up. Now that I look back, I took the easy way out. Dipa did not and that is why she is a champion in more ways than one.

Vimal Mohan

I first met Dipa Karmakar in 2010 at the national camp of gymnastics for the Commonwealth Games in Pune. We were doing a series of stories on the medal prospects for the 2010 Games in New Delhi. In gymnastics, my team and I were primarily focusing on Ashish Kumar and a few other male gymnasts. During that time, Indian gymnastics was languishing in obscurity. However, Jim Holt, an American coach of the Indian team, saw great potential in India's male gymnasts, particularly Ashish. On the other hand, he didn't think much of the women's team, often discouraging them, hurting them in the process.

During one of our visits to the gymnastic camp, one of the Indian coaches advised me to shoot Dipa doing some exercises. He said, *"Watch out for this girl, sir. She is too good. As of today, nobody can beat her at the national level."* Dipa failed to reach the podium at the 2010 Commonwealth Games, and I must confess, like everyone, I too conveniently forgot about her.

Four years later, in the camp for the 2014 CWG, Ashish was a big star. He had created history in 2010 by winning medals at CWG and Asian Games in Guangzhou, China. Every newspaper and TV channel wanted a piece of him. Dipa, on the other hand, remained under the radar.

And then out of nowhere Dipa reached the finals of the CWG 2014 in Glasgow. And the rest, as they say, is history. Not only did she become the first Indian woman to win a medal at the Commonwealth Games, but she also created quite a buzz in gymnastic circles around the world. Thanks to her death-defying vault named Produnova.

Subsequently, I along with my colleague at NDTV, Suprita Das, met Dipa outside the Athletes Village. I was slowly beginning to grasp the importance of that bronze medal for Indian gymnastics. For me, Dipa's bronze, along with Abhinav Bindra's gold, which he won in his fifth and last attempt, were the two greatest medals for India at Glasgow 2014.

I remember interviewing Dipa in Glasgow, and what struck me the most was her fearless attitude: ready to attempt anything without fearing failure. It reminded me of a famous line in Sanskrit from Kathopnishad—*Kshurasya Dhara Nishita Duratya*—It is like walking on razor's edge. Her dangerous manoeuvre on the vault is in itself an ample proof of her walking the talk.

As a sport romantic, I always had the desire to write on the perseverance of Indian sportspersons, especially those who practice Olympic sports. That only cricketers and Bollywood stars get due credit and some others who work equally hard in their fields go unnoticed is a sad reality in our country. The athletes who fail at the international level have to often fight for their survival, settling for class-III or class-IV jobs.

Aware of the harsh realities of sport in India, Dipa once said to me, "It's not a circus. I want the people of this country to understand gymnastics. Like many other sports, gymnastics too is an art. I hope people would understand that." Her words still ring in my ears, evoking emotions every time I think of them.

What also caught my attention was all the hard work that both Dipa and her coach Nandi sir put in every practice session. "Bimal babu, in gymnastics there are no off days.

Every time you have to be more than hundred per cent fit. This game is different. Unfortunately, no one understands it," Nandi sir would often tell me.

The desire to bring marginalised sportsmen to the forefront is what drives me. My work in the field of covering sport has also made me realise that nothing is individual in sports. Every success story has a number of unseen factors behind it.

Of course, those factors work in the background and never, or seldom, get highlighted. So, writing about a brilliant athlete of a marginalised state, of a marginalised sport, was a challenge that I was never going to let pass.

This book is an effort to trace the history, the untold stories, and genesis of gymnastics in Tripura through the real hero of the sport. Dipa Karmakar's personality is similar to that of millions in this country and abroad, and inspires me both as an individual as well as an author. I am sure that she will continue to inspire the youth in this country for years to come.

Vimal Mohan

THE LEAP OF FAITH

Thank God for free Wi-Fi.

The Olympic Village is a very lonely place. Sportspersons from around the world come together to share this personal space once every four years. And for these four years, every national-level sportsperson in every country hopes to be the one who represents his or her nation at the Olympic Games. For some of those sportspersons, representation is secondary; they come here to stand on the Olympic podium. But as is the nature of this beast, the margins between victory and defeat are mostly so fine here that everyone remains on a knife-edge all throughout their stay at the Village.

Usually, there is a tendency for teammates to bond together and take the pressure off each other. The girls from the wrestling team were always hanging out together, the Indian women's hockey team players were always seen with each other. And even the female athletics squad was usually tagging along together, either to practice or to the dining hall inside the Village. I had no one except my coach, Bishweshwar Nandi. We both were the only two representatives from the sport of gymnastics in the Indian contingent at the 2016 Rio Olympics. Nandi sir and I had ventured out together on this journey more than a decade ago; he knew me inside out. He knew all about my mood swings and fiery temper, but this time, instead of being the calming influence that he always is, he too was a bundle of nerves.

They say that the athlete is the cornerstone of the Olympic movement. Well, as an Indian athlete, it can be difficult to believe this, considering the hurdles we have to face on a daily basis back home. But at the Olympics, you do feel on top of the world. And to top it all, there is free Wi-Fi.

Nandi sir had banned me from using my mobile phone. All phone calls back to India were routed through his. Not that he had a local number in Rio; in fact, most of the Indian contingent hadn't felt the need to take local numbers. Technological advances in these four years had made WhatsApp the preferred mode of staying in touch for us, and others, taking advantage of the Wi-Fi in our rooms.

The internet helped release the pressure at Rio; to be more precise, it was watching *Comedy Nights with Kapil* on YouTube that did it for me. I am not one of those who love listening to songs or prefer watching a movie—perhaps it is the way I am, but get me near a comedy show and I am hooked. Nandi sir, too, had been converted along the way, as whenever I felt he was really worked up I would switch on my tablet and get him to laugh. Now, sir is old school; for him Johnny Lever's comic scenes are a touch more appealing than Kapil Sharma's brand of comedy. But he laughed nonetheless. And at Rio that was enough.

The pressure was building. The first week of the Rio Olympics promised much but India did not have a single medal in its kitty. Jitu Rai had reached the final of the men's 10 metre air pistol on the first day of the Games but didn't win a medal. Abhinav Bindra, a man whom I respected and looked up to, finished fourth in the men's 10 metre air rifle, missing out on a medal in a tie shoot. The night before my final, the mixed doubles pairing of Sania Mirza and Rohan Bopanna lost in the semi-final of the tennis competition against the American pairing of Venus Williams and Rajeev Ram. Our lack of medals was the talk of the entire contingent but I was confident that we would return with a few. I knew that India had won medals at the previous two Olympics in wrestling and I was somehow confident that PV Sindhu would do something special. I had met her at the departure ceremony in Delhi and was fascinated by her demeanour since then. Not once did she look hassled and whenever I bumped into her, she would always be warm and would not display any anxiety. Those are positive signs, especially at the Olympic Village.

No one expected much of me at the Rio Olympics. India and gymnastics aren't the same as India and hockey or India and shooting. However, I had created a bit of history on the second day of the Olympic Games by qualifying for the final of the vault. It had sort of made me a mini celebrity in the Indian contingent; and as the days went by and the medal drought continued I became a beacon of hope for many. Asian Games gold medallist Seema Punia met me the night before my final and said, "Dipa, you are a star. Put on the Indian news channels and you will know. They are equating you to gymnastics to what Sachin Tendulkar is to cricket." I didn't know what to say. Here I was, this young girl from Tripura who had always been away from the limelight, the daughter of a Sports Authority of India coach and here my fellow athletes were comparing me to one of the greatest sportspersons this country has ever produced. I did not have a phone, so I was sort of insulated from all this talk. But as the competition day approached, there were reminders of what was at stake. Bahadur Singh sir, the athletics coach, met me the same night, and said, "*Arre, is gudiya se shuru hogi India ki medal tally.*" (This young girl will start India's medal rush at Rio). Nandi sir had tried to keep me away from such talk, but it was inevitable and difficult to escape. India had pinned its hopes on a girl who had never faced such pressures of expectations.

The fourteenth of August, 2016, was a sunny day in Rio but I wasn't disturbed by the sunlight gleaming into my room. I slept well and woke up at seven when the alarm on my phone started to beep. I knew though what to expect. I opened the door of my bedroom to find Nandi sir pacing up and down, it seemed as if *he* were in the final of the Olympic Games and not me. I always did the Produnova vault first, both in practice and competitions. For the final though Nandi sir had decided for me to end with the Produnova. His fear was that I would forget and make a mess of it with the entire world watching. I was pursuing a Masters Degree; could have been trusted to remember at least this much! To get him to relax I searched for my tablet and found a clip of Kapil Sharma's show and got him to watch it as I slipped into my room to get ready.

That morning, I must confess, I was eager for it to end. I had waited a week to compete at the biggest stage in world sport, I was getting restless, but more importantly, I wanted to have an ice cream as soon as possible. It had been far too long and the temptation had only grown with each passing day. The dining hall at the Village had an ice cream counter and I had forced myself to look the other way every day, some days just pinching myself not to look towards the dessert counter. One cannot afford to pile on the inches, especially in gymnastics.

We had undergone a terrible experience on our first day of competition and were caught unawares, this being our first time at an event like the Olympics where one can get overawed. We had spent an entire day during my qualification round without any food or water, as we were not carrying Brazilian currency at that time. This time though, we were ready. It was important for us to eat a heavy breakfast as my final was scheduled for the same afternoon and Nandi sir categorically insisted that I needed the extra energy to cope with the anxiety and nerves that would hit me when I stepped out into the arena. While I knew what had to be done, the same could not be said about him. His breakfast was just a slice of pizza. To be honest, through all of our stay at the Olympic Village, Nandi sir's main course was always a slice of pizza. I kept asking him to experiment and try something new, but even though he was not showing it, he was rather anxious. All through the previous night, he had been receiving calls from back home in Tripura. He allowed me to speak with my parents but that was it. It was he who took calls from the then chief minister of Tripura, Manik Sarkar, and the then state sports minister, Sahid Choudhuri. Naturally, the pressure of expectations was beginning to tell. Nandi sir actually lost three kilos of weight during the Rio Olympics. It is but natural for that to happen, when you do not eat much, not even a glass of juice through the day. I did not have such issues. I am a foodie. I had a bowl of cornflakes and milk, a piece of chicken, topped up with a bowl of yoghurt. For good measure, I picked up some fruits and packed it in my bag. I knew that it was going to be a long day and as I walked from the dining hall towards the transport arcade, the tension started to mount.

For the last two years, since my breakthrough at the Commonwealth Games in Glasgow, I had been dreaming of standing on the Olympic podium. One of my favourite avocation was to watch the Olympic final of the vault on YouTube. I remembered each and every vault of the eight finalists from the Beijing Olympics of 2008 to the London Olympics of 2012. Vaulting is a very difficult discipline to predict as the standings change with every effort. I had qualified in the eighth place for the final and was not expected to run the medallists close. Nandi sir though hoped against hope, as he kept telling me right from the build-up to the final that I needed to get two proper vaults in and that it would put me in contention. I too did not want to finish last. Nandi sir had set a target for me—the Olympics would be a success for us if I managed to come fifth. But he always added the rider, "Anything can happen, Dipa, so give it your best shot."

The best shot though didn't seem to be working that morning. After warming up, all eight finalists headed to the main competition arena. Usually, all the gymnasts train in a small gymnasium next to the competition hall and then proceed straight for competition, but this time it was different. We were Olympic finalists after all, the final eight who had survived the brutal competition and got this far. An hour before the final, we were given a chance to train on the same apparatus that would be used in the final. Even the three reserve gymnasts trained along with us. One never knows; anyone could slip or pick up an injury while landing, and an Olympic final has to have eight competitors.

I tried as hard as I could but I just could not get into my rhythm. Nandi sir looked pretty disappointed on the sidelines. The mat, where we run at full speed towards the board, was very narrow. All of my concentration was focussed on getting the steps right so as to hit the board in sync, to get the elevation required to launch off the vaulting table. But since it was pretty chaotic that morning, as everyone seemed to be in a rush to get as many vaults as possible, and I am someone who prefers some breathing space and no crowding along the mat, it was not happening for me. Such was the rush that my competitors were pulling the mat even as I hit the board. I was rather scared, as just a tiny fraction of movement could have me lose my footing and hurting myself. I decided not to take the risk and walked up to sir to tell him so. I wasn't too bothered about practicing at the empty competition arena, as I knew that nothing would prepare us for the atmosphere and the frenetic cheering from the fans when we returned for the final. As expected, sir was not happy. In fact he lost his cool and started giving me an earful. "Dipa, everyone is preparing here. What is the need for you to go and prepare at the other hall?" I am stubborn and I too didn't budge. But at the back of my mind I did feel that if the final did not go according to plan and I messed it up somehow, then I was in for one massive yelling. Nandi sir had his reasons, I had just done four vaults and had not done even a single Produnova, which was my speciality, and which both of us knew was the key to success in the Olympic final.

Off I went to the other warm-up hall and managed to get some uninterrupted time to clear my head and get my rhythm back. Soon the rest of my competitors trooped in and the announcement came to get ready for the final. That sparked off a rush and I quickly went to the changing room to get into my costume. All gymnasts have to look presentable while competing and whilst the other finalists had support from their staff, who assisted them in getting ready and for applying make-up, I had to do mine myself. Not that I knew what I was doing, I just managed to dab some foundation on my cheeks and that was it. My friends, fellow gymnasts from India, who had been in touch with me the day before had insisted that I use some lipstick as well and having remembered their advice, I looked at myself in the mirror and got it done with.

Nandi sir was standing at the far corner of the gymnasium and since I was ready in about fifteen minutes, I sneaked in a Produnova on the vaulting table in full view of my competitors, who were getting ready. It felt nice getting a good firm landing, the uneasiness of an hour before was gone. I was ready.

Nandi sir came running over and said, "That's it! No more vaults. Everything is perfect and you will do well." The call then came for the eight finalists to line-up. We were just moments away from our fate. But it ended up being a long wait as a bit of history was created just before our event. Diego Hypólito, in what was his last Olympic Games, won the silver medal in the men's floor routine, while Arthur Mariano took the bronze medal. Both were Brazilians and this was the first time that Brazil had won Olympic medals in the sport of gymnastics. As you can expect, they were the toast of the crowd and they took their time lapping it up. There was no way that the organisers would asking them to step off, so we had to wait.

There was a massive cheer as we walked in, perhaps a hangover effect from the celebrations of the last twenty minutes, but in all honesty I didn't really register it then. I was deep in thought and focussed on what I had to do. I was only thinking of getting the first vault to be perfect. Only after my vault was over did I realise that there was a huge Indian presence, cheering me on. I spotted Rakesh Gupta, the chef-de-mission of the Indian contingent, sitting near the vaulting table and that did cause a few butterflies in my stomach to suddenly make an appearance. I told myself, "Dipa, everyone is here. If you do not pull this off, then everyone will laugh at you."

Nandi sir knew what was going on. He immediately stepped in and started the process all over again. He made me stretch and jump to loosen the muscles and kept talking to me, going over the minute details of how we had planned to execute the two vaults. Once your name is called, there is no time, you head off towards the opposite end and then begin the vault and then immediately head back for the second attempt. There is no time to consult the coaching staff, so this was all I was going to get from him. "Remember, Dipa," he kept telling me in Bangla, "we have changed the order of the vault." I was fed up of being reminded non-stop but it was his way of lightening up the mood and getting me to ignore the nerves that were starting to build up. I must confess that even at that stage I perhaps did not realise the gravity of what I was about to accomplish. I was the first Indian gymnast who had qualified for the Olympic Games, and in a few moments I was going to be the first gymnast who would be competing in an Olympic final for India.

Despite vaulting being an extremely technical event, it is easy to break down the process that a gymnast goes through. The preparations begin the moment you put powder on your hands for grip. Then the long walk to the end of the run-up area, a distance of eighty-two feet with the width of the mat being a mere three and a half feet. At the top of the run-up area, we thankfully get a hushed silence from the spectators as we gather our thoughts. At that point, the focus is entirely on how to execute the vault. Years and years of practice and muscle memory lead up to this intense moment. One misstep and it can go completely haywire. You have to run nearly eighty feet towards the table, hoping to be in perfect sync as you hit the board that launches you towards the table. Even as that happens the legs and hands are instinctively swinging into position; the hands usually bracing for impact on the table for the somersault and then the landing. It's over in the blink of an eye, all that perfection in just a few seconds at best. Usually the gymnast knows where they are as they descend, and finally the legs come together for the landing, which is the most crucial bit.

Nandi sir forbade me from looking at the rest of my competitors as the final began. But I managed to sneak in a few glances, as I was not one of the first. North Korea's Hong Un-jong got us going in the final. She was one of the contenders as she had won gold in the 2008 Olympics and was also the 2014 World Champion. The previous year, she had won silver at the World Championships in Glasgow and was also the reigning Asian Games Champion. She knew that she had to come up with something special to defeat America's Simone Biles who was the hot favourite for the gold medal. Her first vault saw her score 15.400, which was an excellent start. But she needed a really high score to challenge Biles and she went for broke, attempting the triple-twisting Yurchenko, which is one of the most complex vaults, and has a difficulty level of 6.300. I think she was the first to attempt it at the biggest stage possible but unfortunately for her, she landed on her back and ended up with a score of 14.400, which effectively ruled her out of the reckoning. I felt really bad for her, as she is one of the best exponents of the vault, but at the same time something stirred inside of me, telling me that perhaps a chance had opened up for me as one of the medal favourites was out.

Canada's Shallon Olsen was the youngest member of the Canadian gymnastics team at Rio. At just sixteen, she had qualified in the sixth place for the final but she too had a disappointing outing. I really wanted to see Oksana Chusovitina perform next but Nandi sir made me turn away. The Uzbekistan gymnast is a legend of the sport and at forty-one, she was the oldest competitor in gymnastics at the Olympic Games. Like India's Leander Paes, she was competing in her seventh consecutive Olympics, having won a gold medal at the 1992 Barcelona Olympics. Along with me, she was the only other competitive gymnast to have landed the Produnova, present at the competition. She had not attempted the vault during the qualification routines but I knew that she was going to begin her final with the Produnova. I had seen her practicing it during the warm-up.

I really wanted to see her attempt the vault but wisely Nandi sir came in between my desire and me and I could only follow Chusovitina's attempt through the reaction of the crowd. I was grateful for Nandi sir's intervention because had I seen the attempt, it would no doubt have stayed on my mind and impacted my thought process for when I stepped up for my vault. Chusovitina executed the Produnova perfectly but could not accomplish the desired landing; she rolled over on to her back while landing. The 'oohs' of the audience told me what had happened and I was happy that another one of my great rivals had not had a remarkable final. It meant that my destiny was in my own hands.

China's Wang Yan and Switzerland's Giulia Steingruber were the next two gymnasts to compete but I was no longer interested in how they performed. My initial curiosity had given way to a determination to deliver and not commit mistakes like my fellow competitors had early on. I was also trying to stay warm. The competition hall was extremely cold and I had walked in straight from the holding area in my costume without wearing a track suit, as I should have.

I was the sixth gymnast to compete in the final and after Steingruber completed her two vaults I was up. Nandi sir looked at me and wished me good luck. All our training over the years had built up to this moment. He had invested so much time and energy in me, perhaps more than in his own son. He always knew what to say and as I set off he told me, "You will do well, I know. I am your guru." I touched his feet and he then left to adjust the beat board before the vaulting table while I quickly walked towards the opposite end. From that point on I was on my own. I could not even communicate with him. We had devised our own non-verbal communication methods over the years. I looked up towards him and he inquired if the beat board was okay. I wanted it shifted slightly towards the left so I touched my head on the left hand side in the pre-agreed way. Had I wanted it pushed back then I would have pushed either of my legs backwards in the direction I wanted the board to be positioned. Satisfied with the position of the board, he waved back and came down to the technical area.

I was on my own. My first vault was the Tsukahara with the 720 degree turn. It was the same vault I had attempted in the qualification round, while this time I was going to begin my Olympic final with it. The vault is named after the Japanese gymnast Mitsuo Tsukahara who had performed it for the first time in 1972. Generally, the Tsukahara refers to any vault where the gymnast uses a handspring with a half body turn towards the vaulting table.

The light flashed to green, which meant that I had thirty seconds to complete my first vault. My entire attention was focussed on that beat board that was there at the distance. At that point, no one thinks of a medal or for that matter even a perfect ten. I raised my hands to acknowledge the judges, took a deep breath, mentally went over the technique that I had to execute, and took a few steps. I then stopped to look up, found the target, the beat board, and after a pause of a second or two, I set off.

The vault was completed in just about six seconds. I landed on both feet but took a step back for support. Nandi sir later told me that it was the best Tsukahara 720 vault I had ever executed. He was up on the mat in a flash, patted me on the back and asked me to concentrate on the Produnova as I made my way back to the start of the run area as the judges deliberated on my score. The judges called it at 14.866, which was a marked improvement from my score in the qualification round. By this time Nandi sir had set the beat board and returned to the technical area behind the judges table. I knew from habit that he would be praying deep within to God for me to land the vault perfectly.

I saw the replay of my first jump and then saw the score that flashed on the large electronic scoreboard. I was very happy with the score and knew the job was half done. Contrary to popular perception, I was not overawed by the Produnova. Having done it thousands of times in practice, it was my 'go-to' vault and I knew, come what may, I would land on my feet. There had been a lot of talk ahead of the final about Chusovitina and me attempting the so-called death vault. Many asked me about it as well, which used to upset Nandi sir as he felt that negative thoughts could creep in and affect my focus. But there was nothing to worry; I was always in control while doing the vault and always had a smile on my face when I was asked that question.

I kept talking to myself as I waited for the light to go green. I kept telling myself to keep my legs straight, as the slightest of angles could veer me off course. The light turned green and I didn't wait too long as I knew what had to be done and I thundered down the mat. I hit the beat board perfectly, the position of my hands were right for the elevation off the vaulting table but my legs were not as straight as I wanted them to be. I thought that I could have landed better but it immediately changed to one of relief. I knew as I jogged off the mat that I would not finish last in the final. I had achieved my goal. Nandi sir came rushing up the stairs from the technical area and hugged me. I could make out from the excitement in his eyes that I had done it. He put his arm around me and took me down towards the athletes' area while a few other finalists congratulated me along the way. I was happy, but I wanted to hear it from him. "Are you happy, sir?" I kept asking him. "Yes, beta, I am more than satisfied," was all he kept replying. "We have achieved what we came to do in our very first attempt," he kept repeating.

We stood side by side waiting for the judges to score the vault. I saw the replay of the Produnova on the large screen and immediately regretted the landing. I knew I could have done better and hoped that there would not be a significant deduction in the points. Finally, the score flashed on the scoreboard: 15.266 was the verdict, once again better than the qualifications. It made me the second gymnast to breach the 15-point mark that day. Steingruber had the lead with an average of 15.216 from her two vaults while I was in the second place with an average of 15.066. A massive cheer erupted around the stadium and I finally noticed the many Indian fans with the Indian tri-colour. Naturally, they seemed to think I would end India's medal drought at Rio and were celebrating. But I knew at that point that it was over. I turned to Nandi sir and told him that I was certain I would finish out of the medals. I knew that there were two other gymnasts to follow, the World Champion Maria Paseka from Russia and Simone Biles from America. I knew that they could easily go past my score. I was not disappointed but was extremely happy. My personal target was to avoid finishing last while Nandi sir had told me that he wanted me to finish inside the top five. Both our targets had been achieved. But he had not yet given up hope, as he thought that we could still end up with a medal if either of the final two gymnasts committed errors. We had seen it earlier in the competition with Chusovitina and Un-jong. But it did not matter for me. For the first time in my career I had breached the 15-point barrier and that too in an Olympic final.

My gut feel proved to be right. Paseka delivered two consistent vaults and moved into the first place with an aggregate of 15.253, just ahead of Steingruber. At that point I knew, even though everyone back home and in the stadium prayed, that I would only finish fourth. In the form that she was in, Biles was never going to make any mistakes. She was supremely confident and was going for her third straight gold medal of the Rio Olympics. Both her vaults were right on the money and she ended up with an aggregate score of 15.966. She became the first American to win the vaulting gold at the Olympics. I finished fourth, just like Abhinav Bindra and the pairing of Sania Mirza and Rohan Bopanna earlier in the day. Paseka took the silver while Steingruber took the bronze, ahead of me by just 0.150 points.

Celebrations broke out in the athletes' area. The American coach celebrated with Biles; Paseka and Steingruber hugged each other. A few coaches came up to Nandi sir and myself, and commiserated with us for having come so close. We picked up our bags and headed towards the Mixed Zone, where the athletes are to face the media, on our way back to the changing rooms. There were a few people from the Indian media there, while the rest were all from international media houses. The questions came thick and fast at Nandi sir. Most of them revolved around the sudden emergence of an Indian gymnast. Many of the journalists had spent years covering our sport and were taken aback at seeing an Indian just narrowly missing the Olympic podium. One question got him very angry. He was asked how he could train me considering we came from the north-east, which was a hilly region. It is a perception that has dogged us all these years. Yes, Tripura is a state in the north-east and there are hilly areas in the state, although Agartala, the capital city, is as flat as the plains in central India! I later saw him smiling. All these previous years, seldom did anyone write about us, and here the world's press was trying to find out how I emerged from a hilly area in India. Not sure whether they were trying to find an analogy of mine with Tarzan as I definitely did not learn gymnastics jumping from tree to tree or one mountain top to another. I learnt it in a gym like every other gymnast in my city of Agartala. I too lost my cool once when an Indian journalist asked me why I did not do two Produnovas as it would have pulled up my score and ensured a podium finish. I glared at him and asked him if he knew anything about gymnastics. Almost everyone seemed to ask me if I was gutted on missing out on a medal but I was seriously not concerned, as by my standards I had overachieved. There were better gymnasts than me in the final but on that day I outperformed most of them. It was a personal triumph but not the one India wanted.

I headed off to change and by the time I emerged, Nandi sir had managed to get hold of the official result sheet. As I came near him, he asked me, "Do you know how close you were to a medal?" I was not aware till he informed me that I had lost out by a mere 0.150 points. At first I was stunned. Till now I was happy with my performance, happy for living up to the expectations of my coach. But when I realised how close I had been, something inside me snapped. The emotions came pouring out and I started sobbing inconsolably. Seeing me, even Nandi sir could not hold back and his eyes welled up. We both sat there sobbing and while everyone headed off to see the medal ceremony, we took advantage of it and quietly headed out of the arena to catch a bus back to the Village.

Luck was however not on my side that day. It took a while for the bus to leave the competition arena, as there were timetables that were being followed. Just before the bus left, in walked the bronze medallist Steingruber. She still had the bouquet of flowers in her hands but mercifully, the medal was tucked away inside her bag. I am sure I would have broken down had I seen it around her neck. My eyes were red but I felt happy for her. I used to follow her competitions through the year and she was one of my favourite gymnasts. She probably knew what I was going through and kept a distance.

We bumped into Sindhu and the national badminton coach Pullela Gopichand the moment we entered the Village. Sindhu had taken a huge step towards winning a medal by beating Canada's Michelle Li in the final Round-robin game of the women's singles and qualified for the knock-out stages. That very morning the 2012 Olympic medallist Saina Nehwal had crashed out of the Games in what was a huge upset. Both Sindhu and Gopichand sir understood the pain I was going through and tried to cheer me up, saying that luck had not favoured me.

At that point a thousand things were going on inside my mind. I kept asking myself if I could have done anything differently. In a situation like this, the mind instantly jumps to conclusions, finding ways to search for excuses and I had fallen prey to it. Even Nandi sir could not escape the post-mortem analysis. All of this plunged us deeper into gloom.

In a bid to cheer me up, he offered to take me to the McDonald's outlet but I wasn't in the mood. I still had to speak to the electronic media outside the Village and tried my best to regain my composure. Finally after a few hours I felt that I could handle the inevitable round of quick-fire questions that were to follow and steeled myself, convincing myself not to cry in front of the cameras.

But you know how these things go, as one can only adjust for a while. Then you hear the same introductions again and again. 'A historic moment for Indian sport.' 'An Indian has finished fourth in the Olympic Games.' 'Dipa Karmakar has just fallen short of a heroic performance.' That did it. When I heard it for the umpteenth time, I just could not control myself. I am not sure if it was on live television, but red spots appeared in my eyes and the tears just didn't stop. I headed back to the room and later my father, Dulal Karmakar, called on WhatsApp. He tried cheering me up and said the same thing: "Do not cry. You have created history." By then I had had enough. "What history, baba? I missed the podium. I would have made history had the tri-colour been unfurled in Rio for the first time."

INDIA'S GYMNASTICS CAPITAL

Tripura? Where is Tripura? Are you from Assam? Are you from Bangladesh? Isn't Tripura a hilly state? How did you manage to learn gymnastics there?

These are questions that I have faced throughout my career. For some, these would be insulting; but we, the people of Tripura, are by nature simple people. Over the years we have always found innovative ways of answering these questions. Like this one: "Tripura, that small state next to Bangladesh, below Assam."

Tripura is considered a frontier outpost as far as Indian sport is concerned. Perhaps the logistical distance from the capital city New Delhi is to be blamed. Not just sports, Tripura and the other north-eastern states are generally also not covered much by the national media. I do get asked a lot about our long-serving former chief minister, Manik Sarkar, but that is as good as it gets. There is much more to Tripura than Manik sir and Dipa Karmakar!

There is just one road that connects Tripura to the mainland, the National Highway 8. The easiest way of getting to Agartala is by taking a flight from either Kolkata or Guwahati. Both these routes fly over Bangladesh. In fact, if you peer out of your window while flying in to Agartala, you will notice the international border fence seconds before touching down at the Agartala Airport. A twenty-minute ride from my house in Agartala will get you to the Integrated Check Post where you can walk over to Bangladesh if you have a valid visa. Due to recent train services being launched, Agartala is now connected by direct trains to Kolkata and New Delhi. Earlier, we had to undertake a seventeen-hour bus journey to Guwahati and then catch a train on the national network. Getting to Delhi would be a never-ending journey. Imagine travelling for three consecutive days, first on a bus, then on a train—mostly in unreserved compartments, and then post all this, competing.

Yet, it was a hardship that was mastered and endured by generations before me. It is rather ironic that many were surprised when I emerged from Tripura and won the bronze medal at the 2014 Commonwealth Games in Glasgow. Gradually, as the Rio Olympics approached, there was a steady trickle of journalists to my hometown Agartala, to meet Nandi sir and me. It seemed par for the course for them to inquire about the sudden craze for gymnastics in our state. Therein lies the contradiction. Tripura is one of the powerhouses of Indian gymnastics in the country. The state has produced an assembly line of national champions, and for one golden period between 1964 till the 1980s, it even dominated Indian gymnastics. Perhaps, in today's age of marketing and promotions, we sportspersons from Tripura have failed to keep the legacy alive.

The man responsible for building that legacy arrived in Tripura in 1964. Since there was no other operational route back then, he had probably taken the train till Guwahati and then got on a bus to Agartala. Dalip Singh belonged to a family of farmers from Bewal in Haryana's Mahendragarh district. He is known to be and accepted as the Godfather of gymnastics in Tripura.

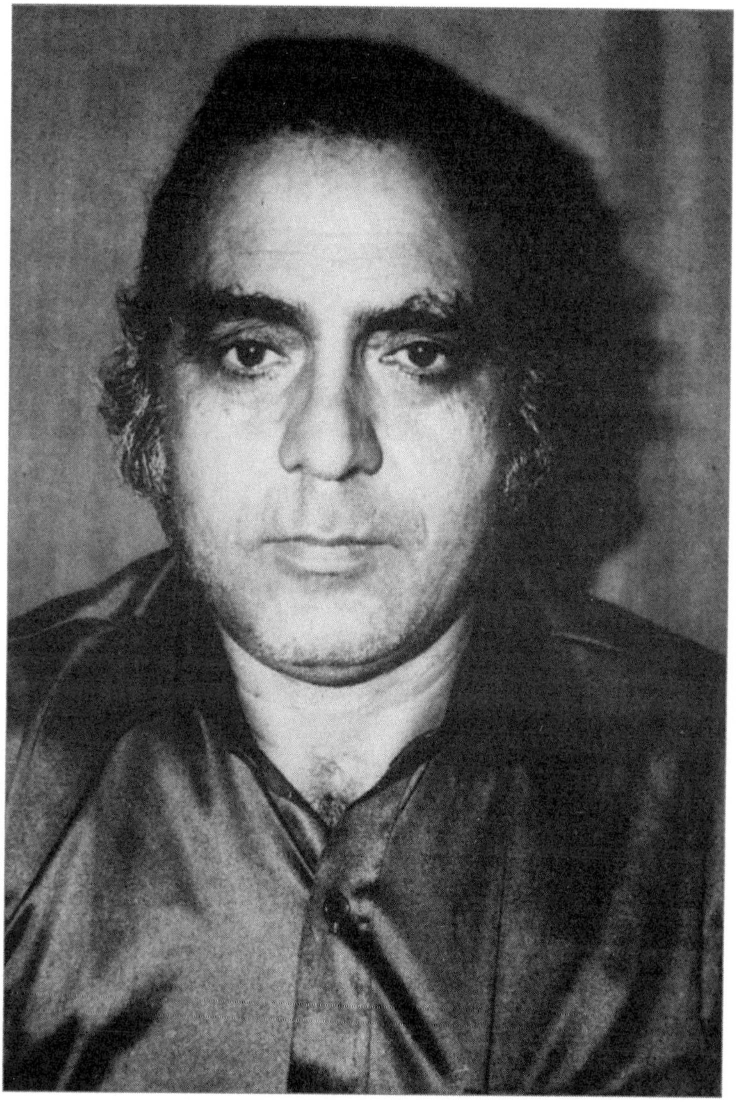

The late Dalip Singh, the man whose arrival made Tripura fall in love with gymnastics.

Like most young men from Haryana, he too joined the Indian Army where he developed an interest in sports. Not much is known about his career as a gymnast but he did represent India in international competitions and later served as an instructor at the Army Institute of Physical Training in Pune. Later, he joined the National Institute of Sports (NIS) in Patiala and was a member of the first coaching course conducted by Russian coaches. On completing his diploma, he joined the institute as a coach.

Dalip Singh was sent to Tripura on deputation by the NIS, following a request from the Tripura Sports Department. At that point, gymnastics was practically non-existent in the state. Sport was actively encouraged in schools and colleges but football and athletics were the only main sports. A few yoga-based postures were largely passed off as gymnastics. The infrastructure too was rudimentary. In the *maidans* or the playing fields, one would occasionally come across scattered equipment like bars and parallel bars that were mostly used for fooling around rather than pursuing serious sport.

The arrival of Dalip Singh changed all of that. He was extremely passionate about his sport and more importantly, he dedicated his life to improve the standard of gymnastics in Tripura. Within a few years, he resigned from his post at NIS and took up a job with the Tripura government. He initially joined as a senior instructor and was later promoted to chief coach, which was the rank of a gazetted officer, after revolutionising the sporting landscape. He loved Tripura dearly and settled down in Agartala after marrying Sushila Devi, who belonged to Manipur. Their house is a five-minute walk from mine and even though I never met him, as he passed away in 1987, his legend has grown over the years and kept alive by the champions whom he identified and groomed, which includes Nandi sir.

Sports in Tripura in 1964 was not even remotely close to the national level. There were no state-level competitions; rather we had various school-level competitions across subdivisions, and teams were selected from there and sent to sub-junior meets in India. Remember, Tripura was a Princely state that merged with the Union of India in 1949, further becoming a Union Territory in 1963. It was only in 1972 that Tripura attained the status of a full-fledged state.

Following Dalip Singh's arrival, a coaching camp was held across various sporting disciplines. There were many other coaches present at the camp as well—it can be compared to a talent hunt that we have these days. One of the sessions conducted by him was to put the students through some basic gymnastic sessions. Being a gymnast himself, he knew the qualities and physical attributes that a good gymnast needed and selected around ten students. Thus began Tripura's formal initiation into the sport, with Dalip Singh conducting the first-ever specialised coaching camp for gymnastics.

He selected four of the most talented boys from that camp and decided to field them at the sub-junior nationals in Bombay, as it was known back then. Since he had a 'services' background, he decided to first hold a mini camp in Pune, at his old training school ahead of the sub-junior nationals. That ten-day camp proved to be an eye-opener for the four gymnasts. They were competing against the best and fittest sportspersons from the Indian Army. It instilled belief in them and also helped them in overcoming their initial shyness. All of them had travelled out of the state for the first time in their lives—travelling to the western coast of India was practically unheard of in those days. Like me, they too were asked if they were from Bangladesh, as not too many people had heard of Tripura.

Bharat Kishore Deb Burma, a distant member of the erstwhile Tripuri Royal Family, wrote himself into folklore when he won the gold medal at the Bombay sub-junior nationals in the floor exercise. Deb Burma also won a bronze medal in the vaulting horse, as the event was known in those times. It was the first instance of a sportsperson from Tripura winning a national-level medal, which brought forth massive celebrations across the state when the news reached back here from Bombay. The government announced a holiday across all schools in Deb Burma's honour. When he returned, there was a huge procession where he was taken all over the city in an open jeep. The foundation of Tripura's success in gymnastics was laid by that triumph, and the adulation that Deb Burma received drew more children to the sport of gymnastics.

For Dalip Singh, this was just the start. He was an extremely large-hearted man who went out of his way to encourage his wards. Mr Deb Burma fondly remembers the time when Singh sir used to take them all out to restaurants in Bombay. Very often he would end up spending money from his own pocket as he tried his best to keep his students well-fed. Even back in Tripura, he would help out needy students with some extra money, pay for them to buy milk or a portion of *mishti doi* or sweet curd after lunch. His wife Sushila Devi knew about his largesse and she didn't mind either. She knew gymnastics was his first love.

Mr Bharat Kishore Deb Burma at his residence in Tripura.

The first Gymnastics camp organised in Tripura in 1964.

His next big find was a young gymnast by the name of Mantu Debnath. Debnath used to frequent a wrestling *akhada* near the Vivekananda Byamagar. Seeing his physique, he was taken by a family friend to meet Dalip Singh and thus began his journey in the sport. Debnath was just twelve when Deb Burma won the gold in 1965. That sparked something inside of him that made him eager to see the new hero, the new champion who had just won Tripura its first gold medal. Debnath was in the crowds when Deb Burma returned, and seeing the adulation and the frenzy, he decided that he too would become a champion one day.

When it came to sports, the Vivekananda Byamagar became the most sought-after place in Tripura. The state had fallen in love with gymnastics and most parents wanted their children to train under Dalip Singh at the Byamagar, whereas earlier he would go door-to-door and coax parents to allow their children to come and train with him. He had personally supervised the installation of the gymnastics equipment at the Byamagar, which meant that scores of champions were bred out of that basic equipment.

Yet Dalip Singh wasn't satisfied. He wanted more gymnasts to train. In a bid to boost the popularity of gymnastics even further, he used his contacts in Delhi and with his former Russian coaches to organise exhibition events at the Assam Rifles ground in Agartala. Teams from Russia came down twice and exhibited their skill in front of a jam-packed audience who were seeing foreign sportspersons perform for the first time in Tripura. Later, German and Chinese delegations also visited Agartala. It had the desired effect, the youth in the state were galvanised and the government too backed him to the hilt.

The first gymnastics team from Tripura.

The increasing influx of aspiring gymnasts created logistical headaches. Dalip Singh was the only coach and found it difficult to manage so many gymnasts at the same time. Never one to take a step back, he improvised. He started to train his fellow physical instructors and passed along the basics required to train beginners. Apart from coaching gymnasts, he started coaching the coaches as well, widening the base of instructors. Deb Burma, his first famous ward, and his fellow teammates, who represented Tripura at the Bombay sub-junior nationals in 1965, were recruited by the sports department and pressed into service. They were sent from school to school to conduct two-week basic camps for students. Those who showed an aptitude for gymnastics were immediately tapped and added to the talent pool. My coach Bishweshwar Nandi was scouted by Deb Burma himself at one such camp in 1971.

Even as the talent pool grew, there was triumph after triumph at the national level. Debnath turned out to be one of Dalip Singh's most famous trainees. He was technically perfect, a skill drilled into him during hours and hours of practice by his guru. He was an excellent all-rounder who mastered all the apparatus apart from the Roman rings. Debnath was on his way to become a record seven-time national champion and in 1975, the first sportsperson from Tripura to be selected for the Arjuna Award. That period was the golden era of gymnastics in Tripura. Every national competition saw gymnasts from Tripura dominating the field. The only man who stood up to the might of Dalip Singh's wards was West Bengal's Nimai Kanji. He was the master of the floor exercises and try hard as they could, Debnath and his teammates found it difficult to beat him and would mostly settle for second place in the floor exercises. The rest of the events were theirs. It is estimated that in that period, across all age groups including the senior nationals, gymnasts from Tripura won over sixty-five gold medals along with eighteen national team titles.

Debnath emulated his hero Deb Burma by having his own procession in an open jeep across Agartala. He was part of a cultural exchange team that toured Kazakhstan, which was after a team from Russia visited Agartala in 1968 where it was decided that there would be a reciprocal visit the next year. Debnath, who was still a junior, won the gold medal in the vault to become the first sportsperson from Tripura to win an international medal. Nandi sir was one of those who were inspired by that feat; he later trained himself under Dalip Singh and went on to win five national titles.

Kalpana Debnath was one of Dalip Singh's most accomplished female students. She created a new record when she won all the titles at the 1978 Surat nationals. She was chosen to be the 'Best All-Round Female Gymnast of India' a record nine times in her career. She also became the second gymnast after Debnath to be bestowed with the Arjuna Award in the year 2000. She too had been sucked into the change that was sweeping Tripura at the time. Her eldest sister, Niyati Debnath, was part of the first women's team to represent Tripura at the nationals.

It was a very different scenario back then; while there was no apparent differentiation between the boys and girls who had landed up at Dalip Singh's stomping grounds at the Netaji Subhas Regional Coaching Centre or NSRCC, not too many took the girls seriously. Not him though. Dalip Singh was someone who was extremely passionate. At times, he would lose his cool and throw out those gymnasts who made mistakes in class. Usually, it was followed by some harsh words which also meant that the offended gymnast would then not turn up for the next two or three days. On the third day though, there would be a knock on the door and Dalip Singh would be there himself, eventually convincing the kid or the parents to send them back for classes. That was his dedication.

In 1968, the first all-girls team from Tripura was sent to compete at the nationals in Ropar. Niyati Debnath was a member of that team, along with Pranati Modak, Shikha Bhowmick, Neelima Singh Roy, Mina Dey, and Sheuli Roy. As expected, they did not set the tournament on fire as for many of them this was their first time at a competition. They did not have appropriate costumes, and wore lowers that were ill-fitting which in turn did not contribute to their scores. But it was the start of something special; it took a while, but the tide gradually began to turn and the women started to overshadow the male gymnasts of Tripura.

Kalpana Debnath was a pioneer among the female gymnasts of Tripura. Her initiation into the sport happened while she used to accompany her sister Manika to the NSRCC. Gradually, she too was bitten by the gymnastics bug and turned out to be one of Singh's most distinguished wards. She led Tripura to many national titles, be it in the individual or team event categories. Her first triumph came at the Junior Nationals in Agartala, her home turf, in 1974. That began an amazing streak for her as she won multiple national titles from then on, and also the gold in National Games in Hyderabad in 1979. But despite her success, she would only be mentioned in newspapers and at school assemblies, and never be honoured with a parade like the ones held for Deb Burma and Mantu Debnath.

That feeling of differentiation existed at the national level too. Debnath was in the Indian team to be sent for the 1974 Asian Games in Tehran. The women's team got their vaccination shots as was required then and even attended a customary pre-departure party, but at the last moment, they were not cleared. When it came to sending teams for exposure trips abroad or cultural exchange programs, it was always the men or the boys who would be sent. Despite Debnath's domination of national gymnastics, she seldom got an opportunity to compete overseas and retired from the sport after winning her final national title in 1979.

Tripura State team for the 1981 Nationals. Coach Mantu Debnath is in the centre in the white tracksuit, Nandi sir on the bottom right.

The conveyor belt dried up after Dalip Singh's untimely death in 1987. By then, most of his wards had left the state, many employed with government departments while some joined paramilitary forces under the sports quota. Nandi sir was one of the few who returned, as he gave up his job as an inspector with the BSF and returned home to become a coach in the sports department under the man who had given him a break all those years back, Bharat Kishore Deb Burma.

Nandi sir's student Banasree Debnath won the gold at the National Games in Bangalore in 1997 and ensured his place in the history of gymnastics in Tripura. Reading this unending roll of honour would perhaps give you an impression of a well-oiled machine, churning out champions at will. The will to succeed was there, although without the equipment the rest of the country had. We trained on basic apparatus, almost all of which was made in India. It was only post the 2007 National Games in Guwahati that the decision was made to transfer the equipment used in the gymnastics competition to Agartala.

Rio 2016 will always remain a special memory. We came here relatively unknown, we almost pulled off the impossible.

One last practice attempt before the start of the all-round competition at the Rio Olympics.

Competing during the qualification phase of the Rio Olympics.
I scored 12.866 on the beam.

I was in breach of the IOA's costume regulations during my qualifying routine. The costume provided by the IOA's official kit sponsors did not fit and I wore an old one. Thankfully they did not take any action.

I did not have a very good score on the uneven bars. I finished in the low seventies but I just had to get through all the routines.
My main target was the vault final.

My moment of reckoning. The vault final at the 2016 Rio Olympics. Eventual gold medallist Simone Biles of America can be seen looking on in the bottom of the picture on the left side.

Pin-drop silence in that massive arena as I attempt the Produnova. Everyone, including my competitors, are watching the Indian attempt the 'death vault'. The judges awarded me a 15.266.

My first vault in the Olympic final was the most difficult one. I knew I had to land a good vault to be in contention. They scored it at 14.866. It was a good vault but not good enough to win the medal as the final scores revealed.

No sadness as I prepare to say goodbye to Rio. I never expected to compete at the Olympic Games and a fourth place finish was beyond my dreams.

MEET THE KARMAKARS

A five-minute ride in a rickshaw from the Radha Nagar Bus stand in Agartala, or at the most a ten-minute walk through a not-so-busy road with houses on both sides and the occasional pond, will bring you to Abhay Nagar and our ancestral house. It is not difficult to spot, as fans and local community clubs have put up posters of Nandi sir and me outside the house. Very often we get visitors ringing the doorbell, wanting to meet me after seeing those very posters.

As you enter the compound you will find an old house made of tin on the right. You have to walk past it to reach the new two-storeyed house that my father, Dulal Karmakar, built. He was born in that two-roomed tin house in 1957. His father, my grandfather, Sukumar Karmakar was a blacksmith and he ran his business from a room at the front of the house. Today, there is a bustling colony in front of our house but in those days there used to be a huge vacant ground or maidan as we call it. Like all young boys, Baba (my father) would sneak out there every evening to play.

Financially, they were not very well off and my grandfather insisted that Baba had to study and get a good job when he grew up. He was a very stern man and no one in the family dared to suggest anything to the contrary. Not too far away from our house is the Nazrul Smriti Vidyalaya, a Bengali-medium school where my grandfather enrolled Baba for his studies. Many years later, history repeated itself as Baba enrolled me in that very same school. But while I joined the school to ensure I got time to attend practice sessions—I had started my career as an aspiring gymnast—Baba's first initiation into the world of sport began at the Nazrul Smriti Vidyalaya in Abhay Nagar.

One of his classmates was Lalit Chakma who was a very promising junior gymnast. Chakma won a medal at the Junior Nationals in gymnastics in the late sixties and it turned out to be a career defining moment for Baba. On his return, Chakma was felicitated by the school authorities in the morning assembly and a holiday was declared in his honour. The euphoria of getting a holiday out of nowhere is something every school-going child will relate to and Baba was no different. But when he came home, it struck him that if for a classmate a holiday could be declared, then why not for him? Since gymnastics was the 'in thing' in Tripura those days and Chakma too was a gymnast, Baba decided that he too should swim with the tide. Remember, this was the era of Dalip Singh, and Baba got together a few friends and landed up at the Netaji Subhas Regional Coaching Centre or NSRCC.

At that point, everyone was welcome and Baba and his friends enrolled at the centre hoping to be gymnasts. There was not much interaction with Dalip Singh. True to his Army roots, he was a very strict man and not many had the courage to walk up to him and strike up a conversation. Baba was just a school-going boy and his interactions were limited to the coaches who assisted Dalip Singh at the centre. But he soon fell foul of the strict regime imposed by Dalip Singh for no fault of his, which brought an early end to his fledgling gymnastics career.

My grandfather was pretty firm when it came to his studies; it was non-negotiable and left Baba no choice. Every day, when he returned after school, he'd have a bath, eat something my grandmother had cooked, and then set off for the long walk to the NSRCC. His other classmates though would skip school by the end of the fourth period in order to reach the Centre for the evening session, which got underway at three. Baba would only reach there well past four and be taken to task almost every day by the coaches who thought he was having a jolly good time roaming the city instead of being present along with the rest of his friends. His defence of completing school fell on deaf ears and gradually Baba started getting disillusioned with this daily admonition. Perhaps it was fate that the gymnast from the family who stood out would shine a generation later.

Not too far away from the NSRCC is the Vivekananda Byamagar. In Tripura, every budding sportsperson with a certain amount of talent makes the journey from the Byamagar to the NSRCC. In Baba's case it was the other way round. Now, in Bengal and Tripura, festivals are celebrated with much fanfare and all the young boys are seen hanging around a *pandal* during these times. One time Baba and his friends were invited to the Byamagar for an annual puja of Lord Hanuman and it turned out to be a career-defining visit. He was instantly impressed by the large posters of body builders and their impressive and toned physiques adorning the Byamagar and decided he was done with gymnastics.

The late Bansilal Sinha, an officer with the Oil and Natural Gas Corporation of India, was one of the leading officials at the Byamagar and a resident of Abhay Nagar. Through him, Baba and his friends, who were all from the same locality or *pada* as we say here, got enrolled at the Byamagar after paying a princely sum of one and a half rupees. The monthly fee for using the facilities at the Byamagar was around eight annas or fifty paisa, which my grandmother would hand over every month to my father. There was no time-bound schedule at the Byamagar, as being a member one could use the facilities whenever one wanted. Of course, my grandfather was not in favour of this, but since Baba was giving his full attention to studies, there was not much he could do.

Over the years, Baba developed into a fine weightlifter, no doubt helped by an early start. As his body weight increased, he dominated all the age groups he took part in. He was adjudged the best weightlifter of Tripura when he was in Class X. And even though the medals started to pile up at home, my grandfather never failed to remind him that these were useless and that he needed to get good marks in school. But the moment Baba would leave the home, my grandfather would show the medals to his friends and show off his son's accomplishments. He also allowed Baba to enrol his youngest daughter, my aunt, in swimming classes that were being conducted by a family friend. Thanks to Baba, we were on our way to becoming a sporting family.

Baba did not stop there. He was the state champion in the 52 kg category, then in the 56 kg category, the 60 kg, and finally the 66 kg category. Overall, he was undefeated in all the state championships he competed in for over a decade. Even today,

Baba's record in the 56 kg stands as the Tripura state record. To this date, he very proudly tells all his acquaintances that it stands at 85 kgs in the 'snatch' and 112.5 kgs in the 'clean and jerk'. It remains his regret that he could never win a National Championship medal despite participating every year. Back in those days, travelling to the Indian mainland was an ordeal. I connect with his pain and anguish, as years later I too undertook the same painful journey on many occasions. More on that later. Baba's last competition was the national trials ahead of the 1982 Asian Games. He had completed his graduation by then and was under pressure from his father to get a job. As the only son, Baba too wanted his father to stop working and there was a younger sister to be settled as well. For a few years, he tried his luck in Tripura, coaching young weightlifters and helping out the State Weightlifting body before a friend suggested that he apply for a formal coaching degree.

His background in sports meant that he had a head start and was accepted for a year-long course at the Netaji Subhas National Institute of Sports in Patiala in 1985. My grandfather had been forewarned by his friends that letting the only son of the house travel to North India for a year could lead to him breaking free of the shackles that had been imposed on him since his childhood. My grandfather was worried that Baba could end up falling in love and getting married and he was having none of it. He agreed to Baba going to Patiala on the condition that he first get married. So, just before his departure to Patiala, Baba got married to my mother Gauri, who was a college student from South Tripura. He then left for Patiala while Ma (my mother) carried on with her studies.

Upon completion of his course, Baba was immediately offered a job with the Sports Authority of India. My grandfather was overjoyed; it was a government job after all and it suited everyone. Baba did not want his father to work, he was getting old and he had been ailing for a while. The family income wasn't much but a steady government job was what anyone wanted in the mid-1980s in India. Baba's first posting was in Behrampore in West Bengal and he moved there with Ma. My elder sister Puja was born in 1988 and that led to another showdown between Baba and his father. My grandfather was very attached to Puja and could not bear to be away from her. He ordered Baba to leave the job and find something suitable in Tripura. Baba was quite perplexed, as these jobs were difficult to get a hold of and he was not inclined in any way to leave a government job. Soon, Baba realised what the problem was and he sent Ma and Puja back to Agartala and that was the end of it. There were no more complaints from my grandfather and Baba was then briefly transferred to Manipur and then to Udaipur in South Tripura, which was a two-hour drive at best from Agartala. That suited him and he would shuttle between his family in Agartala and work in Udaipur.

I was born on 9th August 1993.

GROWING UP IN AGARTALA

There was a pall of gloom in the family when I was born at the Indira Gandhi Memorial Hospital in Agartala, and my birth did nothing to lift it.

My grandfather had passed away three months before, rather suddenly. He had a history of high blood pressure, and one day he complained of uneasiness. Baba, who was staying at home those days—making the daily fifty-kilometre journey to South Tripura, took his father for a check-up to the local hospital. The doctor found nothing abnormal and asked him to come back a week later for another round. But my grandfather never completed that second check-up. He collapsed in the hospital while waiting for his tests, and by the time his wife and his grandson, my elder aunt's son, could fetch a doctor, he was gone.

Those were the days before mobile phones and even basic telephones were inaccessible, and there was no way of contacting Baba who had left in the morning as there was some urgent work to be attended to in his office. He, however, had a premonition that all was not right and returned on his own after signing the attendance register in his office, unaware that his father had passed away. It was only when he returned home and saw the crowd assembled outside that it dawned on him that something was wrong.

The family coped with the unexpected demise and Baba being the only son was now the head of the family. Ma was expecting me and there was something to look forward to. But even that wasn't without any drama.

I was born a few days ahead of schedule as Ma had to be rushed to the Indira Gandhi Memorial Hospital in Agartala after a small incident at home. She had gone with Baba early in the morning for her weekly check-up, and the doctors had declared that all was well. A few hours later, while she was busy drawing water from the tube well in the house, she slipped and had to be rushed to the hospital as she was in tremendous pain. The doctors decided to go for an immediate caesarean section delivery, which brought me into this world. It was a Monday and I was born at 9:30 in the morning.

My father's first born was a girl and perhaps everyone was hoping for a boy this time. A few family members who were present during my birth could not hide their disappointment when they learnt that Dulal Karmakar was now the father of two girls. "Oh, Dulal! A girl again!" they told him. Thankfully, Baba was not dragged down by this negativity. He was overjoyed at becoming a father again. His one regret in life wasn't that he was a father of two daughters; it was that he couldn't get to wear the Indian colours. My Baba sincerely hoped that one of his daughters would go on and do what he could not achieve, and with the little I have achieved I feel he is happy. Ma always says that earlier, even though there was scepticism and ridicule, now the entire family is recognised by the virtue of being *my* family.

My elder sister was born on the day of Vishwakarma Puja, so Baba named her Puja. There weren't any preparations back then for naming a child in advance, like we see these days. To be honest, it took a bit of time for me to actually get a name. Baba used to call me Guddu, while the rest of the household called me Tina. I do not know how those names came about, but finally Baba decided that it was time to do away with the dual names and he settled on Dipa.

The name Dipa literally translates to light or the enlightened one. I am not sure if I was enlightened but I was definitely very stubborn growing up. I am not going to recount most of the instances here, perhaps someday you could grab hold of my elder sister and get her to open up on what she had to go through. Ma says that I wasn't a very quiet child, I would always be running around the house, and my favourite pastime would be running to the gate, opening it, and standing on the road to watch the rickshaws and especially the horse carts that used to ply in Agartala. I also had a particular affinity to the tube well inside the compound, the same one where Ma had slipped just before her delivery. I would love getting wet and playing with water, perhaps it had something to do with the climate, and I loved drawing water from the tube well.

I have a really bad temper and more often than not Puja bore the brunt of it. It didn't matter that she was five years elder to me. Despite my frail size, it was I who dominated the usual fights between sisters. I once flew into a fit of rage and slapped her extremely hard, while another time I gave her a hard kick that really put her into much discomfort. Everyone at home thought that Puja had broken her leg, as she kept crying and wailing, while I seemed oblivious to the mayhem I had unleashed. Ultimately, I had to stay clear of Ma. Baba was mostly never at home as he kept getting transferred a lot. Both Puja and I were safe when he was around, or else Ma would give us a good scolding if we were up to some tricks. More often than not, it was I who was on the receiving end, and I usually ran to hide behind Baba whenever he was around, knowing that he would always rescue me from any predicament!

As I grew a bit older, I started getting accustomed to the daily routine at home. Puja by then had already been initiated into the world of sports. It was a given with Baba's background that both of us had to play a sport till a certain level. But Puja, in fact, got away much easier. My parents had enrolled her in Yoga classes and she had a private coach who came and taught her once a week. Her coach was a state-level gold medallist but even that didn't exactly motivate Puja to twist her body into various postures. Perhaps, my parents made a mistake selecting the day for those classes. The Yoga teacher would come every Sunday, you see, and getting a young seven- or eight-year-old kid to focus on any activity on a Sunday was arduous. It was the day when everyone was at home. There would be cousins over and the house would be bustling with activity. Puja was more interested in playing with us and would find ways of trying to get out of her classes. Her usual modus operandi was to play with us through the day and fall asleep just before the Yoga instructor would come around. Gradually, he too figured out that this wasn't heading anywhere and he quietly told Baba and Ma that there was no point wasting time. Puja, by then, had been enrolled into an English-medium school where it was very difficult pursuing sporting ambitions. The focus there was entirely on studies and the teachers were usually much stricter; they didn't look the other way when it came to excusing one for sporting pursuits. That was the end of Puja's nascent sporting career and it meant that when the time came, I had to be the one to follow in my father's footsteps.

There was a nursery school near our house and at the age of three, I took my first steps towards an education. When the time came for admissions into a proper school, Baba decided to enrol me at his alma mater, the Nazrul Smriti Vidyalaya in Abhay Nagar. Baba knew from his experience with Puja that if I had to get involved in a sport, then I could not do so at an English-medium school.

Baba was well aware of the rich history of Tripura in gymnastics; he had himself briefly flirted with it in his younger days. One day he decided that it was time for me to begin my initiation into the world of sport. There was nothing dramatic about it. I was over five years old and he told me one evening that I was to go with him the next day to meet someone. That was it; he didn't tell me who we were to meet or where we were going. The next day I sat behind him on his scooter and made the short trip to Vivekananda Byamagar, Baba's old gymnasium, where I met his colleague, Soma Nandi. That was the day my gymnastics career began.

The Vivekananda Byamagar is the breeding ground for future champions in Tripura. Every successful gymnast that the state produced after Dalip Singh began the coaching module, has at some time trained at the Byamagar. Yes, the nearby NSRCC was where the elite gymnasts trained but the Byamagar is an integral part of the history of Tripurian gymnastics.

The Byamagar is first and foremost a private club. Baba had been a member of the Byamagar since 1976; it was where he fell in love with weightlifting. The Byamagar is a single storey structure with an asbestos roof that is divided into two sections. As you enter the compound through the gates, the first section is the gymnasium to the right, which is where you will find equipment that is largely used for the power games. Through the day, you will find enthusiasts lifting weights and trying to chisel their bodies into perfection; a poster of Arnold Schwarzenegger would not be out of place at the Byamagar.

The second section, divided by a small partition, is the gymnastics area. Again, nothing fancy here. Old equipment has been crammed into this small space, mats lie everywhere, piled up wherever space permitted, some of which that cannot be used anymore. Then again, there is no disposing them. Even a mat with foam sticking out can be put to use at the Byamagar. Right next to the entrance to this section is a small area bereft of any equipment. It is here that the coaches and the staff at the Byamagar lay down the mats on which the children practice. At times when there is a sudden influx of extra students, especially during the holidays, the narrow confines became inadequate. The coaching staff then lays out the mats at the unkempt garden in front of the building. It is quite a sight to see children, as young as five years old, trying to do a handstand or a somersault onto the mat as music streams in from the gymnasium in the next room where, through the open windows, one can see some serious pumping of iron. The two worlds peacefully coexist in the Byamagar.

The late Haripad Chakrabarty was the secretary of the Byamagar in the 1970s; he was very fascinated by the gymnasts being churned out by the state under Dalip Singh. He appealed to the Tripura State Sports Council to start a gymnastics centre at the Byamagar and they agreed. It suited them just fine, as there was no extra cost involved apart from providing the necessary equipment that you still see here. All the cost of running the Byamagar was the club's. The salaries for coaches were paid for either by the Sports Council or the Sport Authority of India depending on who was posted there by either organisation.

In 1998, Baba took me to Byamagar for the first time. I did not know then, but the reason he chose the Byamagar and not any other sport for me was because of Soma Nandi. Soma Nandi was my first coach; even today I must confess I am very scared of her and I am more at ease with her husband, my current coach Bishweshwar Nandi. Both Baba and Soma madam were colleagues, both were coaches with the Sports Authority of India, and they both had worked together in Udaipur in South Tripura. It was to her that he entrusted me.

Soma madam too was a gymnast. At the age of five, she had enrolled at the NSRCC and eventually become a coach with the Sports Authority of India after calling time on her career. For the majority of her coaching career, she taught the basics of the sport to every child who enrolled at the Byamagar. It requires a lot of patience, as children at the age of five aren't used to following authority or commands from coaches, being free-spirited. I am in awe of Soma madam and her team for soldiering on every day, knowing full well that there is a high attrition rate. Initially it is good fun but as one grows up and gets to senior school, the demands of modern education have the two-hour practice sessions give way to private tutors. Grades are more important than a sporting hobby. I was not the only promising gymnast to enrol under her during my time there; there were a few others who were equally good and were dedicated to practice. The only difference was they discontinued after a few years.

For any trainee at the Byamagar, there are a few basic exercises that they have to start with. Nothing fancy. A normal forward roll, a backward roll, cartwheels, front turnover, back turnover, and the split. Almost every child in India does these exercises in school. The difference is doing them once a week during the Physical Training period and doing it every day under the watchful eyes of the coaches.

Contrary to what has been written about me after my Rio performance, I did not exactly fall in love with gymnastics from day one. For me, it was something that was new and every child at the age does take some time to get used to the new set-up. I used to go every day to the Byamagar after school, spend a few hours there, complete the exercises, and return home. I was too young to understand what was going on but it did give me great satisfaction coming home and telling Puja of what I had done that day at practice.

More than the practice, I had a fascination for the equipment at the Byamagar. I was particularly keen to master all of them and despite my size, would look for an opportunity to be able to sneak in a minute or two either on the uneven bars or the vaulting table. One day Soma madam saw me eyeing the uneven bars and threw me a challenge. Perhaps she had seen the determination in my eyes to master the technique. I have this streak of stubbornness in me, right from my childhood, and usually get my way if I want something. That day there were three of us at the Byamagar. Soma madam challenged us to mount the uneven bars using the Upstart technique. It involves transferring yourself from a swing below the bar to a position above the bar. It is a fundamental skill in gymnastics but I am not sure why she expected one of us kids to do it. If any of us managed to execute the Upstart, the prize would be a piece of gum. A Big Babol chewing gum! It may seem trivial, but for a child there is nothing better than maxing a challenge and then boasting about it the next day in school or at home. With great determination, I pulled myself up to the bar using all my strength and I was the only student that day who could rise to the challenge. As promised, the next day she handed me a Big Babol chewing gum. That piece of chewing gum was my first award, and while it may not have been gold, but back then it was all that mattered. I distinctly remember saving it till I got back home and showing off my prize to Puja.

Gradually, the frequency of chewing gums began increasing at home. It was a good inducement for a kid and I slowly started to enjoy these little challenges where each little win was a step in my becoming a full-time gymnast years later. There was a flipside to the chewing gums though. Back in those days, each piece of gum came with a small sticker inside the packet. Both Puja and I loved collecting those stickers and we ended up sticking them on a steel almirah that was in one of the rooms. Over a period, that entire almirah came to be covered in these stickers with miniature photos of dolls and dragons. It really caused my father to flare up one day when he discovered what we were up to. Both of us sisters got a massive scolding. That almirah, though, is still there in the house and so are the stickers on it.

The Byamagar was slowly becoming my space. It was one place where I could be on my own and didn't have to share with anyone. When Baba was not in town, Ma would come to the Byamagar to pick me up in the evenings. I made it very clear to her that I did not want her to see me during practice. Other parents would come inside the complex and watch their children but not Ma—she had to wait outside. With Baba it was a different story. He was a member of the club and would drop by to have a chat with Soma madam, but for Ma I had drawn the line and never once did she try and cross it. It must have been a task for her to come every day and stand outside the Byamagar, filled with curiosity, but she religiously followed it through all the years of my training, whether it was at the Byamagar or even when I moved to the NSRCC subsequently. Ma probably saw me practising for the first time inside a gymnasium just before my departure for Rio. She would never feel bad or take it to heart, and I would get her to stop on the way back at some fast-food joint. Agartala is known for its street food and I absolutely loved eating rolls and puchkas, or golgappas as it is known throughout India.

As the years went by, I started to get more and more involved with my practice. Over the years the Byamagar had produced many good gymnasts who had gone on to represent the state and win awards. I too wanted to emulate them and win medals. My idol was Banasree Debnath, who was the toast of the gymnastics scene in Tripura when I started. Debnath ended Tripura's barren run at the national level in 1997, by winning a gold medal in the balancing beam at the National Games. She had created a flutter by executing a front somersault on the beam at those games. It was a Category D manoeuvre, which she did twice in the finals at Mysore. She told us that she knew she was to win the gold medal when she landed perfectly on the beam after the first attempt. I too wanted to win like her and seeing the endless hours of practice she put in, served as motivation for me.

Banasree was the person I wanted to emulate in gymnastics. But then, I am my father's daughter as well. I had another idol growing up. I watched Karnam Malleswari win a bronze medal for India at the 2000 Sydney Olympics on TV. Naturally, it was a huge thing especially in our house with Baba being a weightlifting coach. That euphoria lasted a few months and Baba even took me to a weightlifting centre in Agartala to show me what the sport was all about. The Durga puja pandals in the city, all had photos of Malleswari, which obviously made me excited. There used to be an iron rod in our house in Abhay Nagar. One day when Baba wasn't around, I tied a sash around my waist like I had seen Malleswari wear on TV, called my cousins and friends, picked up the rod and announced, "I am Malleswari."

FROM NANDI TO NANDI

My first major medal came on the balance beam. Yes, it will surprise most people. The vault was not exactly something one could realistically hope to master at the Byamagar. The lack of space meant that it was impossible. But in between the fun and games, there was always a serious competition going on—to be better than the rest. Plus there was my idol Banasree Debnath, who had won her national gold on the beam. So rather instinctively, the beam was the apparatus that I mostly trained on. Little did I know at that young age that my first medal would also throw my life upside down.

In 2001, there was a North East Sports Festival in Agartala. The competition was amongst sportspersons hailing from the seven north-eastern states of India, and one of the sports was gymnastics. I would have been around eight or nine at that time and I was selected for the Tripura state team. Of course, most of my teammates were much senior and elder to me and I just about made the team for the beam and floor events, while being on reserve for the rest. It was a new experience for me. All sportspersons taking part in the festival had to stay in a hostel. What fun for an eight-year-old!

The hostel wasn't too far from my place and Ma used to come visiting every evening to see if I was okay. I remember not doing well in the floor exercises on the first day of the festival but I more than made up for it by winning the gold medal on the beam the next day. I was too young to realise it, but it made a lot of people sit up and take notice. No one, not even I, ever believed that I was going to win it. I think they fielded me so that I didn't end up warming the bench throughout the festival. I was up against many seniors, some of whom had even competed in the senior nationals. To be honest, it is much later that you start getting affected by the pressure or the weight of expectations. I do not remember much. I just went there and executed the routine that had been practiced and was very excited when I ended up being declared the winner. There was a good reward for me at the end as hostel food is usually not the most satisfying. I went home, ate a good hearty meal, and went off to sleep.

While I slept, a momentous decision on my career was being taken. At the time, Kamal Saha was the secretary of the Tripura Sports Council. He was particularly fond of gymnastics and one of his first decisions after assuming office was to transfer Soma Nandi to the Byamagar, to ensure that the young gymnasts enrolling there had a good understanding of the basics. Saha sir summoned Soma madam to his office and made the decision that took me all the way to Rio, to the cusp of an Olympic podium. "Soma," he said, "Dipa has a lot of talent. She has a good future ahead but I do not think she will be able to rise if she continues in the Byamagar. I am going to shift her to the NSRCC." He did ask her if she had any objections to the move but no one was going to question the decision of a top official.

Perhaps it was destined that I had to move on. For some time now Soma madam had been thinking that the time had come to shift a few girls to another training centre. As we grew and started to attempt more complex routines on the various apparatus, the chances of an accident or a freak injury grew. She needed a male coach alongside her to support the gymnasts but the Byamagar was a small and basic centre and there was never going to be a senior appointed. Keeping that in mind, she agreed, but there was still the resentment of losing a ward to another coach. Perhaps he could sense it, as Saha sir then informed her of the next coach, who would be none other than her husband, Bishweshwar Nandi.

Bishweshwar Nandi belonged to the third generation of gymnasts who were groomed and honed into champions by Dalip Singh. In 1970, he was a young boy studying at the Pragati Vidya Bhawan, a school in central Agartala. As part of Dalip Singh's vision, coaches were sent to schools to identify those with an aptitude for gymnastics. The coach who came to Nandi sir's school was none other than the legendary Bharat Kishore Deb Burma. Nandi sir was among the first set of students who made the cut and then, having made the initial draft, Deb Burma moved on to another school. Two more coaches arrived later, Radharaman Das and Nilamani Dey who gave some more basic training. Nandi sir was selected to undergo formal gymnastics training under Dalip Singh at the NSRCC. There was still one final seal of approval needed. Singh cast his gaze over Nandi sir who was twelve at that time and told the coaches to keep an eye on the boy.

Nandi sir was selected for an off-season camp but he did not have the courage to ask his family for permission. More than his parents, it was his uncle Subhash Nandi whom he was terrified of. Eventually, when he could not muster enough courage to broach the topic, he confided in his coaches. Coach Nilamani Dey visited the Nandi residence, all geared up to convince Nandi sir's family. But he was in for a surprise. The senior Nandi gave his wholehearted approval to the plan and thus began Nandi sir's journey into the sport.

The camp was held for a month at the Basic Training College near the GB Hospital in Agartala that wasn't too far away from his home. Nandi sir made sufficient progress to impress the coaches and after a month, he was informed that he had made the cut and that from then on, he would train under the guidance of Dalip Singh at the NSRCC. Once again, his courage was put to test. He did not have a bicycle in those days and training at the NSRCC meant walking three kilometres one way, daily. The roads were very narrow and there were not too many operational streetlights. He, not too long ago, admitted to me that he felt frightened walking back alone after practice in the evenings, especially because of the presence of stray dogs that would bark and chase down people on the road.

Sir, though, persevered, and over the course of time came to not regret those long walks. He was a fast learner who soon began to win medals in age group competitions that were organised at the centre. Along with the certificates, there used to be household utensils that were awarded as a prize as well and every one at home was pretty happy with that too. Impressed by Nandi sir's promising beginning, Dalip Singh worked his contacts and asked him to fill some forms. He sent those to Patiala, which one fine day brought forth a cheque in Nandi sir's name for a princely sum of three hundred rupees. NIS had a stipend scheme for promising sportspersons, and the recommendation of Dalip Singh, who was pretty well-known there, was never going to be ignored. It worked out to twenty-five rupees per month and just to put it in context, the monthly income of the entire family would have been around a hundred rupees. Over the years, as he grew older and started to win more medals, not just in Tripura but at the national level as well, the stipend also kept increasing. For a period of five years, he was awarded a stipend of six hundred rupees annually, which more than took care of his needs and diet. His performances also ensured that the stipend would be well deserved. In 1975, he won gold in the School National Games and then gold in the Junior Nationals the next year. With sir delivering on his early promise, Dalip Singh turned his attention to getting him a secure job where he could continue to pursue his career without any roadblocks. He offered him advice and told him to either join the Army or a paramilitary organisation, which he could ensure for him. In 1976, at the age of eighteen, Nandi sir was offered a job by the Border Security Force (BSF), which he accepted. Within a few days of joining, he was called up for the national camp that was being held in Jalandhar.

Nandi sir in his official kit ahead of the 1978 Bangkok Asian Games.

It was at the camp under the then national coach DK Tandon that Nandi sir's career started to take flight. The improvement happened in leaps and bounds, no doubt helped by better quality equipment. He was a very disciplined individual and there was never any financial burden as the BSF job took care of that. Nandi sir hardly spent any time working at the office as he was mostly at camps through the year in Patiala.

As his skills improved, sir waited for his first chance to wear the Indian colours. He, along with thirty-one other gymnasts, was called for the selection trials for the 1978 Commonwealth Games in Edmonton. It was a long camp that went on for around four months. After about every month, there would be a trial where the numbers would be whittled down. After the first trial, sir ranked twenty-first and made it to the next phase of the camp. When the next round of trials came around, he jumped to a position just outside of the top ten that put him in the reckoning to make the team. There was one trial left and only four gymnasts to be ultimately chosen to represent India. He threw himself into practice wholeheartedly, hoping to improve his scores to make the team when the final trials came around. But as fate would have it, he suffered a stomach upset the day before the trials. He was in pretty bad shape and pleaded with Mr Tandon to shift the trials by a day so that he could recover. The rules were rigid and Mr Tandon refused to do so, which caused sir to break down. In desperation, he popped a double dosage of the medicines prescribed by the doctor at NIS Patiala and landed up at the venue. He was very good on all the apparatus routines and was considered a master of the pommel horse routine. That day he pushed himself as far as he could and hoped for the best. The trials were held over two days, with two apparatus on the first day followed by four the next day. With just twelve gymnasts remaining, the trials got over by noon the second day and when the results were declared that evening, to everyone's surprise and his as well, Nandi sir was announced as the winner.

Nandi sir with two unidentified participatants during the opening ceremony of the 1978 Asian Games.

It was the first time he would be representing the country, and it marked a full circle for him. It was an NIS stipend that had set him up in Tripura and eight years later it was at the NIS he had been chosen to wear the national colours for the first time. His family back in Agartala did not have a phone so there was no way of relaying the information to them. The fastest way of getting the information across was with a postcard and that is how the news reached Agartala of how Bishweshwar Nandi had beaten seniors like Nimai Kanji and Manjit Singh Panther to top the Indian selection trials. Of course, some were astounded but for the coaches who had seen him from the very beginning, it was on expected lines. From then on he was a regular in the Indian squad and won his first national title post the Commonwealth Games and then repeated the feat the next year as well. He became a national champion for the third time in 1984. Following the Commonwealth Games in 1978, where he reached the final of the all-round competition, Nandi sir was the only gymnast sent for the Asian Games in Bangkok and he reached the final of the pommel horse. Four years later he reached the final in the all-round category at the 1982 Asiad in New Delhi. In six tournaments including the 1982 Asiad, he was named the captain of the Indian team. Twenty-eight years later, I competed in the same arena at the Indira Gandhi stadium in the 2010 Commonwealth Games.

On most occasions he had to return without a medal. This was the case for most Indian sports at that time. It was frustrating but it was difficult to take on the reigning powerhouses of Asia back then. There were barely one or two centres in India that had the equipment that was used in competitions at the global stage. Most of the apparatus in centres across India were sourced from a company in Ambala. Those were basic equipments and it was not possible to improve drastically while using them. Therefore, the few odd results that were achieved were at places like Karachi in 1980 where the Indian team won a gold, and an Invitational Tournament in Iran in 1985, where the team won a creditable bronze.

Nandi sir was called for the camp for the 1986 Asian Games that was held in Seoul but he decided to move on after a few days. He had left the BSF in 1980 and had been living mostly in camps ever since, returning to Agartala whenever there was a break. Most of the expenses at the camp were taken care of, and on top of that there used to be an allowance for campers. When the need arose, money would be sent from home. But after ten years of living that life, he wanted out. At a time when self-motivation alone drives an athlete, there isn't much you can do when one day it suddenly snaps. There is a void that exists, and hanging on to memories will not feed a family.

He had plenty of offers to consider, as he was handed an appointment letter twice as a coach by the NIS, with postings in Kolkata and Lucknow. He had completed his coaching diploma at NIS whenever he stayed there during the years he spent at national camps. The Indian Railways who have supported sportspersons repeatedly offered him employment and so did the Punjab Electricity Board. Private sector companies like the Tatas and Birlas too wanted him to join them under their sports quota but after a decade of being away from Agartala, his mind was made up. He wanted to return home and if possible, seek employment with the state government as a coach and impart the knowledge he had gained over the years to the next generation. Today, he probably would have earned a much higher salary had he taken up one of those lucrative jobs but he was always intrigued by the story of his original mentor Dalip Singh. He wondered why he should seek a job outside the state in gymnastics when his own coach had come from the outside and mentored so many champions and created an assembly line of good gymnasts. That thought kept nagging him and he decided it was Agartala and nowhere else.

Getting a government job though is easier said than done and Nandi sir had to wait for a year and a half before he was appointed as a coach. However, there were always people around who appreciated his pedigree and achievements and they pitched in. Chandan Sen was a prominent leader in the CPI-M government of the day and he ran a football club called Blood Mouth. He asked sir to be the conditioning coach of the team and with nothing else to do, he accepted the role. The money was not great as it was more of a stipend, but it kept him occupied. Twice a day, in the morning and in the evening, he would be at the football ground, charting their progress. Ultimately, it was Chandan Sen who managed to get him the appointment he so badly wanted, that of a coach with the Tripura Sports Council.

There was no escaping the watchful eyes of Dalip Singh who too had been petitioning the government for a job for sir. Having spent most of his life around the gymnasium, and that too a disciplined life, he took some time to adjust to the new job and the freedom it afforded. It was time to be much relaxed, and he would slip away in the middle of the coaching sessions and enjoy a game of volleyball with the other coaches and trainees at the NSRCC. He was spotted enjoying himself on a couple of occasions and on the third time his former coach who was now a senior colleague summoned him.

In no uncertain terms it was drilled into him that he had to follow the same dedication he had while competing in his new career as a coach. For Dalip Singh, being a coach was the most important job in the entire sporting ecosystem. The discipline and standards expected in the players had to be first adhered to by the coaches. Those words have stayed with sir all through his career. Even today he rarely attends a phone call while coaching and does not let any other distractions cross his mind in those two or three hours when he is at the gymnasium.

His first assignment was with the sub-junior boys team, the same age group he was when he was selected to begin his career in gymnastics. Very soon there was a marked improvement in their standards and a few were called up for the national camp. His performance was being noted in the corridors of power and after five years he was transferred to the women's team. The glory days of Kalpana Debnath were long over and there had been no standout gymnast from the state after her retirement. It was felt by the senior officials that with his experience Nandi sir was the right fit to restart the assembly line of female gymnasts in Tripura. Of course, he wasn't too happy and he felt that his job was incomplete, as he wanted to win the senior title as a coach, having won it thrice as a player. His objections were brushed aside; after a point you can't argue with authority. A similar story repeated itself many years later when Soma madam was informed that I would be moved on to a new coach.

His mind wasn't in it initially, but when there is no option available, one has to find a way to succeed. He was already married by then and felt bound by societal norms when it came to being in extremely close contact with young girls. Gymnastics, after all, is a contact sport and it can get pretty embarrassing at times if you are not used to being in close contact with female sportspersons. Most of his career he had spent with the men's teams in Patiala and this new assignment needed a completely different approach. But he managed to convince himself and as is his style, threw himself wholeheartedly into his new assignment. It took a while, a few years, for the results to come but patience is a virtue that coaches must have in abundance. Banasree Debnath was part of the first group of girls who were placed under him and she achieved his dream of winning a senior title by winning a gold in the National Games in 1997. Nandi sir had made the successful transition from a champion to that of a coach of a champion and over the next few years Debnath continued to win titles and medals at national meets. It was into this successful environment that I, a naïve eight-year-old, was about to enter.

Nandi sir receives the tricolour from the then PM Rajiv Gandhi on the occassion of the 40th Independence Day in 1987 in New Delhi.

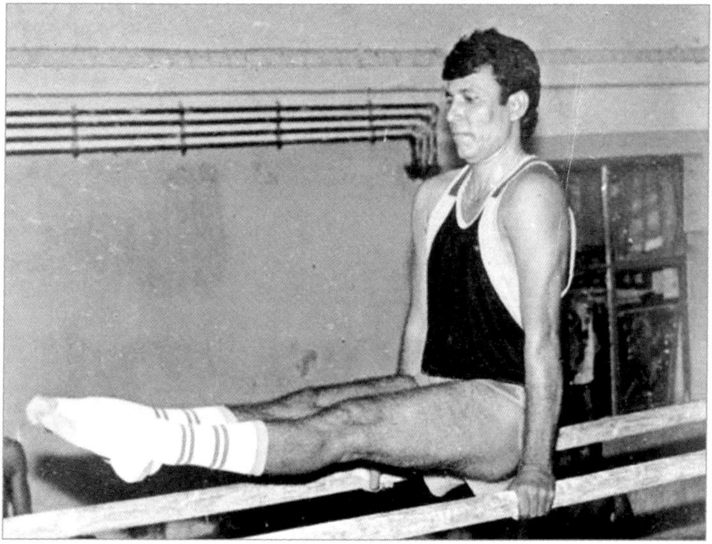

Nandi sir going through a routine on the parallel bars during a national camp before the 1986 Asian Games.

The original Karmakar. Baba ended his career undefeated across multiple weight divisions at the state championships. He regretted never being able to wear national colours and it was his wish that I do so one day.

The Byamagar was once Baba's training ground. He is now the secretary of the Byamagar.

Meet the Karmakars. A rare occasion when all four of us are together. My elder sister Puja, Ma, Baba, and me.

I am a very good actor and I am throwing a tantrum in the yard outside our old house.

A birthday party at our old house, My sister Puja is on my left.

Tripura CM Biplab Kumar Deb visiting the Durga Puja pandal at our home during the 2018 festivities.

The love of my life. My niece Anushreeta Saha (Abu).

A panoramic view of the state of the art facilities at the NSRCC today. I wish I had access to these facilities early on in my career but everything happens step-by-step. Hopefully, Tripura gymnastics will soon regain its pre-eminent position in India.

The indoor stadium at the Tripura Sports School in Badarghat.
I train here when the NSRCC is not available.

An unidentified member of the Byamagar trains alone.
Notice the outdated equipment.

THE JOURNEY BEGINS

I was surprised when the news was broken to me. A part of me felt sad leaving the Byamagar, which had been my playground all these years, but the NSRCC had a charm of its own. All the senior gymnasts used to train there. It was much bigger than the confined space of the Byamagar and I knew a few girls who had preceded me here. Soma madam used to send us on and off to the NSRCC to train on the much better equipment, hence I was familiar with the place. My idol Banasree Debnath used to train there as well, and I used to always try and sneak in a few looks whenever I had the opportunity to visit the NSRCC.

I was too young to miss the Byamagar for more than a few days. A new world had opened up and there was so much to learn and enjoy. But I took an instant dislike to my new coach, Bishweshwar Nandi. I knew he was Soma madam's husband and had seen him occasionally at the NSRCC when I used to go there, but I had never been formally introduced to him. Even though he had heard about me from his wife and my father who was also posted as a coach in the same facility, I was just another young kid who had been thrust upon him. At that point, he was more concerned about winning more senior national titles and I was perhaps more of a distraction.

There were two other gymnasts, Sharmishtha Malakar and Shimantika Debnath who were about my age, already training with Nandi sir. I quickly reconnected with them as we had spent some time together at the Byamagar and soon we were a gang. Sir initially was not too focussed on the kids and he used to spend most of his time coaching the senior girls. We did the same amount of physical conditioning as the seniors but that was it. I used to pester him daily to allow us to try new things on the floor but he was very rigid and I mostly got a negative answer. If we were lucky, we would get a set agenda for the session when we reported for our daily training sessions. He would assign us a set of exercises and would then go on and work with the senior group. In between, he would observe us and shout instructions to correct any mistakes that had crept into the exercises or even something as basic as to keep the knee straight while landing. The lack of doing anything substantial soon got to me and I wanted out.

My partners in crime, Shimantika Debnath and Sharmistha Malakar at the NSRCC.

There were other coaches in the centre and I wanted to move over to train under them. I used to complain a lot to Ma and would rant and rave almost everyday when I returned from practice. But she would always calm me down and tell me to be patient, as she knew that Nandi sir was a good coach. Perhaps she told my father too, and he had a word with Nandi sir. Sir explained to him why it was not possible to allow eight-year-olds to do the same set of exercises and routines that the senior group was following. Baba being a coach understood the concept of load and recovery but being a kid, I wouldn't listen.

There was another reason I disliked Nandi sir. He used to carry a big cane to the centre every day. We used to have a lot of free time during our daily sessions and when he was busy with the senior group, we would be up to some mischief or the other. I was a brat and very often would get into trouble that would see me getting a good whack. I would do the things we were not allowed to do. Monkeying around is the right word actually. I loved hanging upside down from the uneven bars with my legs wrapped around the bars. There were umpteen times when I fell straight onto the mat below. If a routine had been assigned on an apparatus, I would do the opposite and break the flow of the entire group. Sir would threaten that he would beat us blue if we did not stop but I never cared. Another favourite pastime of mine would be to challenge the boys who trained under another coach. I would goad them into attempting back and front somersaults and would then try to match them. That usually meant a scolding or on the days that I crossed the line, a warning tap from that cane. On some days I would complain to Ma but I quickly learnt that it was better to keep shut. Ma knew that I was pretty mischievous at home and if I ever did tell her about a beating that I received from sir, it would be followed by a couple of tight slaps from her as well for being naughty.

Since Ma knew I could be a handful—she usually got to see it every day—and because I could not retaliate against sir, my elder sister Puja was the one who would end up on the receiving end of my temper. Even though she was five years older, there could only be one brat in the Karmakar household. Poor Puja still bears pockmarks on her arm from the multiple times I have dug my nails into her over some trivial matter. If you can call Maggi trivial, that is. I loved Maggi and while Ma would always give both of us an equal portion, I would quickly gobble down my helping and then snatch hers and finish it. It would lead to fights but they were mostly one-sided, if she hit me then I'd hit her more. There have been times when in a fit of rage I have bitten her or actually torn her books. Somehow or the other, I used to get away and rarely did I face the music from my parents. They knew that I had a bad temper and Baba also mentioned it to Nandi sir when I started to train under him.

Over the years my relationship with Puja improved rapidly. Till we were both in Agartala, both of us were competing for the affections of our parents. For me, it was always about being better but when I started to spend time in camps, we started to bond very well as we would both catch up on each others' lives on the phone. She was lonely without me but still had Ma. I used to be alone and that time Baba too was out as he was posted in the Andaman and Nicobar islands. Today, that bond is stronger after the birth of her daughter. We don't fight over Maggi anymore but we do sneak out of home and sample the street food of Agartala once in a while.

I love street food. And very often it got me into trouble with Nandi sir early on. I used to be pretty skinny and he used to always rub it in and tell me to eat well. I used to always retort, *"Mere ghar me maach macchi banta hai,"* which translates to "we eat non-vegetarian food at home", implying that there was no shortage of food at my place. He would complain to Baba as well, and one time Baba got really wild and threatened to burn my costume and stop my training if I did not start eating healthy. That was the operative bit. They all felt that I did not eat; I on the other hand did not know what the fuss was all about as I was always eating. *Poori sabzi* at a roadside shop on my way back from school was a must. And there was a traditional variety of mixture called *chanachur*, which is an eastern speciality. If nothing else was available, there was always Maggi to fall back upon. Ma was very generous with pocket money and on days that I was short, I would come up with some expense needed for school that would be difficult for her to deny or question. Today, as an elite athlete, the first thing that you watch out for is your diet. Oh, I so crave those ice creams and *rasogollas* and the local savouries from Sherowali Sweets in Agartala.

It helped that school was nearby. I was not fond of sports at school and perhaps the only time I took part in any sporting activity was during the annual sports day. What was the point, when you had to leave school every day at two to get to training at three? These days I do try and catch a nap after a session but back then the days were long and hectic. Studies could not be neglected and there were tuitions at eight thirty in the evening after I returned from my training. Baba would always pick me up on his way back from work and there I would be, riding pillion on his LML Vespa, holding on to ensure I did not slip off. My parents were not too concerned about my studies but the warning bells would start ringing if I failed any of my exams. That meant extra tuitions, which added to an already packed weekly schedule. Later on, I would get special exemption from my teachers to write exams at a later date, as they would start clashing with my competitions, especially the half yearly exams at the end of the year. Sunday used to be a rest day and there would be no training. However, that was the day I was supposed to brush up my knowledge and I had three tuitions lined up. The first one was early in the morning and there would be two back-to-back in the afternoon and evening.

Back then, I would pick the tuitions any day ahead of training. You could slack off while doing your mathematics timetables, but Nandi sir would not tolerate any lackadaisical attitude while training. Gradually, as the training started to increase, I realised why he had been such a fine gymnast himself. For him, those two or three hours of training would be non-negotiable. I have mentioned earlier that he was very clear that the body had to be warmed up before we started doing our routines and come what may, we had to do our running, stretching, and basic moves before he allowed us to start with the specifics. He was pretty clear that training meant training on all the four apparatus. Every day, it was the same set routine—the vault, the uneven bars, the beam, and finally the floor exercises. There was no deviation, either for us kids or the senior lot. Once we were finished, there were

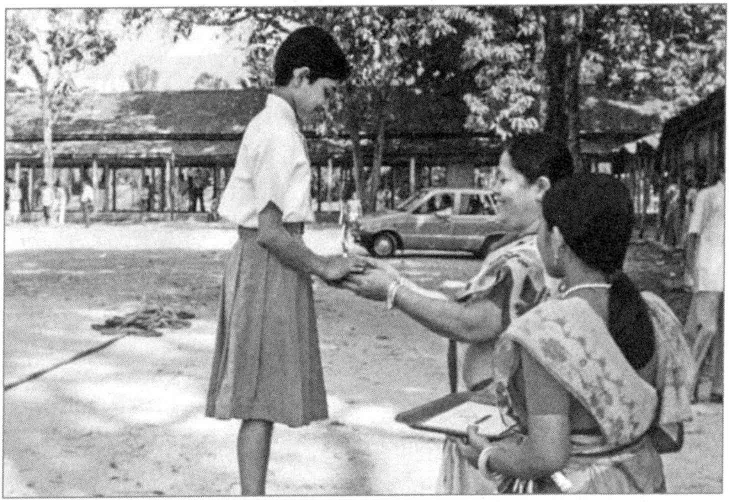

I may not have attended much of school but I won a lot of awards.

Recieving an award from Agartala MLA and now Minister Sudip Roy Burman during an annual function at school.

more conditioning exercises to be done. Rain, harsh weather, or even a power cut did not stop the sessions. Power supply used to be erratic at times and there were numerous occasions when the gymnasium plunged into darkness. The other groups would stop but if we were midway through a session then, there would be no break. A lone tube light would be on, running on backup, which would cast just about enough light for someone to avoid knocking into one of the apparatus and in just that much light, our sessions would continue. It would be a sight, this one group of girls continuing their routines while everyone else just waited for the electricity to return. I am not sure if even sir could make out at a distance of twenty feet of who was doing what. You could laugh at his methods and his unflinching and uncompromising attitude, but these repeated drills were what were helping me improve as a gymnast. Within a few years of moving to the NSRCC, I was starting to be selected for meets outside of the state.

The initial high though, of being selected to travel outside Tripura soon turned into a nightmare for me. I was a poor traveller back then. My first trip was for the School Nationals in Ambala in 2003. Now, these games are mostly held in the winter months and Agartala sees moderate winters at best. I was too young to go alone so Baba spoke to the officials and sent an elder cousin of mine, Shipra, to be with me. But even her presence could not save me from the ordeal that I had to undergo. Back in those days, there was no rail connectivity still and so the entire team undertook a twenty-four-hour bus journey from Agartala to Guwahati. The capital of Assam can get pretty cold and the weather along with the exhaustion started to take its toll on me. There were no rooms waiting for us in Guwahati to stretch our aching limbs or lie down. We hopped on to a train to Delhi hoping to be able to get some rest ahead of our arrival. Even those dreams went up in smoke as soon as we boarded the train. We were around thirty of us and most of the tickets were still waitlisted. There was no option of not making the journey, so we were all told to adjust. The few seats that we had were divided into groups, and some of us younger ones including me had to adjust with two others. It was quite uncomfortable and a few of us slept on the floor of the carriage in that cold weather. Remember, they were not temperature controlled AC cabins but just a normal sleeper carriage which did get pretty cold. It must have been quite a sight for the rest of the passengers to see these young kids all stretched out all over the compartment. The handbooks say that one should head into competition in peak physical condition, none of Nandi sir's conditioning though would prepare anyone for this kind of travel. It was one big adventure for me then but looking back now, it is not something that is advisable for any athlete, leave alone a kid.

We somehow managed to reach Delhi after another arduous journey and most of us had a bath at the New Delhi Railway Station in the waiting room right after. No hot showers for athletes as we are privileged to now, and a cold water bath on a chilly December evening in the capital was all we had. It was a no brainer that I would fall ill. By the time we caught the train to Ambala, I was vomiting.

There was an even bigger shock waiting when we finally got to Ambala at the competition venue. I didn't know what was unfolding, as I had never seen this vaulting horse, as we call it. We trained on old apparatus in Tripura, whereas here was a brand new vaulting table at the School Nationals. Having never trained on one of this design, I was at sea. There was no way to get in touch with Nandi sir and there were no qualified gymnastics coaches travelling with us as well. So the big reveal. In my first ever competition outside of Tripura, at the School Nationals no less, I had a no vault! The rules of the competition were clear that there had to be a mandatory vault for a score to count. I was too intimidated by the vaulting table and when my turn came, I ran at the board, got the elevation to do a handspring but slipped on the table and as I did so, fell down while landing. As the vault was not completed, I got that fine number that excites us gymnasts, a zero. Usually, a high number precedes it, but this time it flashed a 0.00. At least I attempted it despite being sick. I was not the only one intimidated though. There were others who got nowhere close to the board and just ran under the table instead of launching off it.

I was pretty ashamed at my no show and quietly came and sat down with the rest of my teammates. Perhaps I was young or perhaps they knew that I was unwell. Most of my peers only had a few kind words to say and not sarcastic comments that one usually gets when you slip up in competition. Anyway, all that travelling for one zero vault. I do not even remember going out sightseeing considering how sick I was. I do remember heading out to buy a gymnastics costume with my cousin. She was the moneybags for this trip, as Baba had given her some money in case I needed anything. I think we managed to win just one medal on that trip. After it was over, it was the same route back to Agartala. Thankfully, this time the tickets were confirmed. Nandi sir wasn't too perturbed by the result as he said that there was no problem when I informed him of what had happened. "The experience is what matters," was his advice. And he was right; as the first three or four times I competed in national level events, I returned empty-handed.

A year later I was ready and won my first medal at the School Nationals. They were held in Vishakhapatnam and there is an interesting tale from that trip. Not too many of us from Tripura used to win medals. The good old days of Dalip Singh's wards sweeping competitions were long over. Once we all were done with our routines, the teacher accompanying us decided to leave the competition venue and return to the hostel. We all were told to gather our kits and follow her back. I had done my vault and was waiting for the results and didn't want to leave. "No one is going to win a medal, you have done your best and now we must leave," she said. You can't argue with the head of the delegation, so I picked up my kit and joined the rest of the team heading out of the hall where the competitions were being held. Just as I neared the exit the loudspeaker crackled to life. "Results for the vault competition. Gold to Dipa Karmakar from Tripura." Everyone stopped and turned around to look at me in disbelief; I wasn't there. I was already running towards the judges' area and the podium.

BAREFOOT TO NATIONAL CHAMPION

It took a while before Nandi sir was convinced. I kept winning medals at various age groups competitions and also School Nationals, but perhaps he thought of me as no more than a mischievous brat. And how could he have not? Almost every trip I went to led to one *tamasha* or the other. The thing was that I wanted to be everywhere. I wanted to win medals each time I travelled out of Tripura, but I also did not want to miss out on having fun. I was usually in contention at every competition while most of my teammates and the accompanying officials would leave me to head out, sightseeing. Once we were in Mumbai and I created a huge ruckus when it was decided to go and see Shah Rukh Khan's mansion in Bandra. I wanted to go too but had to be left behind due to my event. I won a silver in the vault eventually. But it never compensated for the feeling of jealousy when my teammates related their stories to me. The medal was secondary, Shah Rukh Khan's house was more important.

The turning point in my relationship with sir and his belief in my abilities came at the Junior Nationals in Jalpaiguri in 2007. Nandi sir was starting to pay more attention to us as we grew up. The seniors under him had begun to move on—some got married while others could not make the cut required to move up a gear. Our sport has a very limited shelf life; very rarely do you see the likes of Chusovitina who have been competing since the 1992 Olympic Games. My partners-in-crime, Shimantika and Sharmishtha, did not make the cut as well, as sir did not feel that they could win a medal. So it was just me and a few other boys who were selected, and we all made the trip together with sir. On reaching there, sir decided that it was not right to leave me alone in the girls' wing, so I stayed with them and occupied the pride of the place, the only bed in the room while the rest of them, including sir, slept on the floor.

My first gold medal at the Jalpaiguri Junior Nationals in 2007.

Nandi sir had previously never accompanied me to any competition. And I wanted to show him what he had been missing. Thankfully, it turned out to be a memorable competition for me. I won three gold medals and two silver medals despite hurting my ankle during the floor exercises. One of the gold medals was in the balance beam, and that's where sir noticed me. He later told me that watching me perform that day on the beam convinced him that I could go on and reach the national stage. Later, Soma madam told me that he had called her from Jalpaiguri and could not stop gushing over my performance. Sir had coached Banasree didi to a national title on the beam and knew what was required to win. He was very impressed by my execution and by my ability to not wilt under pressure or be overawed by the sheer size and magnitude of the nationals.

On our return to Agartala, I could see him taking a keener interest in me. Something had triggered off the coach's impulse in him, and he was determined to take me to the next level. A few days after our return, he got word that a few scientific officers from the Sports Authority of India were visiting. He took Shimantika, Sharmishtha, and me to get us assessed by them. It turned out to be a career changing assessment as the scientific officers declared that I had no future as a gymnast.

Nandi sir was stunned, but as they explained their findings it became clear to him why. It turned out that I was flat-footed and that it is extremely rare for a gymnast to succeed in the sport with such an anomaly. It also explained why I had injured my ankle in Jalpaiguri, as the jumping movements are difficult to execute when flat-footed and lead to a lot of pressure on the ankle. There were no such issues with Shimantika and Sharmishtha but I, the most promising of the lot, faced the prospect of having my career nipped in the bud at the formative phase itself.

Sir didn't tell me about it then and thought about a way to extricate both of us from the impending doom. His thoughts went back to his days at NIS during his diploma course, to a class where he had thankfully paid a lot of attention. He remembered being taught that there were exercises that could lead to the condition being naturally cured. A bit more digging around put him on the right track and he found an innovative way to get me involved as well. He got my attention by invoking my ankle injury and told me that it could be avoided if I seriously followed the set of exercises he was giving me. He did not stop practice and neither did he stop me from competing. In a few months from then, I would go on and win at the School Nationals in Agra. I had no clue of the disadvantages of being flat-footed and even if I had been made aware, I was too naïve to know that it could have an adverse effect on my career. Every day at home, at school, and before and after practice, I would religiously do the exercises he had asked me to do. It was fun and I could do it while sitting in class on the bench, or even at home while watching TV. It took a while, but just within a year there was a natural curve in my feet and thus, unknowingly, I had overcome the first major challenge of my career.

There have been significant challenges since then, but none have ever managed to break me. Perhaps it is my resolve; perhaps it is because of my stubbornness or because I can channel my anger in the right direction. I am not one to take no for an answer. Failure drives me on; I seem to do better at the second time of asking. My first National Games in Guwahati in 2007 were a disaster. I did not win a single medal. Nandi sir was furious as he thought that I should have won the gold in the vault as I had reached the final after qualifying in first place. But I made an error during one of my vaults and was docked a penalty point, which saw me finish fourth. Nandi sir carried that hurt through the games. He felt that the judges were biased and subsequently he had many disagreements with the jury led by Kalpana Debnath. Sir was convinced that the scores awarded to me were low on purpose, but there was no way of proving it. I ended up empty-handed in those games and right before returning, sir walked up to the jury and gave them a piece of his mind. He challenged them to wait till the next games and predicted that I would sweep the gymnastics medals at the next National Games in 2011. And when the time came four years later, I lived up to his word, winning five gold medals at the Ranchi Games.

Wah Taj! A visit to the Taj Mahal during a School Nationals in Agra.

That incident brought us closer. Seeing him fight for me made me appreciate his concern. It is very rare to see Nandi sir lose his cool. By nature he is a very quiet sort of a person;

he does not speak much in a gathering and prefers to be a silent observer. But put him in a gymnastics hall or see him sit with fellow coaches or those associated with gymnastics and you will be rather amazed to see the transformation.

For us though, he was a dictator. At the training hall, he was always strict and both of us have had memorable confrontations. He always carried a stick to threaten us but having never used it all these years, it did not carry any threat for us. There was one instance though, when I thought that I was going to get a lashing like never before. At the NSRCC, there are various groups of trainees under a particular coach. Since the number of apparatus is fixed, the coaches had worked out a schedule between them wherein they would rotate their groups every forty minutes. This ensured that every evening, every gymnast would complete the basic set of exercises. You may be an expert of the vault or the pommel horse but in our sport you have to complete the all-round event to be eligible to qualify for individual finals on the apparatus. This one day, I was not having a good stint on the vaulting table. Each time I attempted a vault, something or the other kept going wrong. It is the nature of the sport that you cannot be perfect every day and on every attempt. Sir was watching me from behind but knowing that it was an off day, did not interfere much. However with each attempt, I was starting to lose it. I do get very angry at times and when that happens, I tend to go massively overboard. At home everyone knows about it, but at the NSRCC it did catch everyone by surprise, except sir that is. Turns out, Baba had told him earlier of my anger issues and how I would beat up my sister or cause mayhem at home when angry.

The forty minutes on the vaulting table were up and the next group arrived. I wanted to land one perfect vault and then move on. I ran to sir and requested him to allow me one more vault. "No, Dipa, the time is up and they are waiting for us to complete. Leave it and start afresh tomorrow," he said. I burst out crying and kept pleading with him to allow me another chance. It was quite the scene I was causing at the NSRCC but that stubborn streak in me had taken over. He too realised that no harm would come if I was allowed another attempt and said, "Okay, go on but just one more vault." In the state that I was, there was no way I was going to get a perfect landing. I ran up to him all cranky and pleaded for one more attempt. By this time the other coaches too had stopped training, with the entire din coming from the vaulting table. They were all watching the situation unfold. Clearly taken aback and unsure of how to handle this, sir asked the other coaches to allow me another attempt. Even that turned out to be a very bad vault for me. I tried as hard as I could but the landing kept getting worse.

I ran up to him again and started pleading for another chance. By this time he had had enough. The stern dictator mode was back on and having indulged in my tantrums for a while, he decided to crack the whip. Despite my pleadings and wailings he refused to allow me any more attempts. Something in me snapped. I flew into an uncontrollable rage. Perhaps there was some measure of control, as instead of lashing out at him I kicked the wall, which was a few yards away from where he was standing. Such was the ferocity of the kick that a piece of skin tore out and I started bleeding. It took a moment for everyone to realise what had just happened. There was silence all over that huge gymnasium. Sir was the first to react; he started screaming at me. "I will break your legs if you behave like this again," he yelled. Nothing got to me. I was having a fit and was shaking with anger. I could not even feel any pain in my leg even though there was blood oozing out. No one else moved or uttered anything. At that moment all eyes were fixed on just two people—the one yelling and the other shaking. He kept his distance though, probably careful to stay out of my kicking arc. He knew what I was capable of, Baba had warned him many years ago and those thoughts probably came swirling back from the depths of his memory. He probably feared that he was going to suffer the same fate as Puja.

All of a sudden the dark clouds passed and I realised what had just happened. I was ashamed and I ran out of the gymnasium. The tension sort of visibly reduced in the hall. Sir told his group to take a five-minute water break and sent another girl to look for me. I was outside the gymnasium, looking for a stick. Obviously, she went back and reported that. I found what I was looking for and returned to the hall with a huge bamboo stick. Seeing me with it, sir probably thought that I was going to hit him with it. I could see the apprehension and fear in his eyes as I approached. I walked up and thrust the stick into his hands. "Hit me with this, you have not brought your stick today," I said. He grabbed the stick from my hand and told me to go have water and go home. I went, changed, and quietly waited outside the gymnasium for someone to come and pick me up. I did not utter a word of what had happened; neither did I speak to anyone when I got home. I went straight to my room, refused to eat dinner, and locked myself up despite Ma asking me what was wrong. They immediately knew that something had happened, as I became a recluse only when I had committed a major mistake. Baba called Nandi sir to inquire what had happened. Sir was extremely upset and he relayed the entire evening's shenanigans to Baba. I received a massive yelling from Baba after that, admonishing me for behaving with sir like that.

Later that year Baba got posted to the Andaman and Nicobar Islands. It was a world away and he did not want to uproot his family from Agartala. Before leaving, he had one more important task to do. My performances at the Junior Nationals and other competitions had come to the notice of the National Federation and I was called up to the national camp in Kolkata. It is a prerequisite for any camper to have a passport ready and Baba started the formalities to get me one. The paperwork was done in Agartala but the passport was issued from Kolkata. A few days after it arrived, Baba showed it to one of his colleagues who thankfully spotted a major goof-up. None of us had paid close attention to the specifics and by mistake I had been labelled a boy. Clearly, it was a major cause for concern and Baba knew that it had to be changed before he left for his assignment to the Andaman Islands.

He took me and went to Kolkata where the Regional Passport Office was located. The office opened at ten on weekdays and not wanting to take any chances, Baba landed up with me at seven thirty in the morning. It was a long wait and there were already many people ahead of us in the queue. Finally we managed to get inside and Baba explained the situation to the officer in charge who directed us to a particular counter to get the change done. The official at the counter understood the problem and asked Baba to get his daughter along next time so that the verification could be done on the spot. Baba pointed at me and said here she is. At that point I had a very short hair cut, what we in Agartala called a boy cut. The official, though taken aback, immediately gave the go ahead for the changes to be made.

Having made the trip to Kolkata and back, Baba had to leave for Andaman Islands and there was no one this time around to drop me at the camp which was being conducted at the SAI centre in Salt Lake, Kolkata. Another gymnast from Tripura had also been called up and so the decision was made for us to go together. I had a mobile phone, to be used in case of some emergency. We both landed in Kolkata together, but there was someone present to receive my fellow camper. She decided to go to her guardian's place for the night, and they both put me in a taxi and told me to go alone to the centre. I was pretty taken aback as I had never travelled alone and Kolkata was a big city. I called up Ma to tell her of my predicament and then cut the phone. I did not want the taxi driver to know that I was alone and scared. Ma, by then, had called up Baba and he kept calling me non-stop. I told him that I was all right and then stopped receiving his calls. Thankfully, the taxi driver was a good fellow and he dropped me at the centre without any incident. It is only after I entered the campus that I breathed a sigh of relief and called up both my parents to say I was fine. Baba was extremely upset and he later pulled up my fellow camper for abandoning me in the middle of nowhere in Kolkata.

It wasn't the only time though that I have faced such a situation. A year later I went missing in New Delhi for a while. I had been selected for the Indian team for the World Championships in London and the entire team had to travel to New Delhi for the visa. All of us had to get recent photographs for the application form and there were a few shops near the visa centre. In the confusion I got left behind while the remaining group returned to the centre. Suddenly the coaches realised that I was missing and all hell broke loose. My phone was off and there was no way of contacting me. I did not panic and just waited near the shop knowing that at some point someone would return looking for me. The coaches called Nandi sir and he called Baba in the Andamans to inform him. Both were constantly on the phone, berating the coaches for being so careless and trying to reach me on my phone. After a while I was found and everyone breathed a sigh of relief, myself included.

Getting to the national team was a proud moment for Baba. It had been his dream that one of his daughters wear the national colours. It was his regret that despite so many years of being a sportsman himself, he could never represent the country in the international arena. Initially, I took some time to adjust to the new environment in the camp. It was a new set-up and I had to get used to not being with Nandi sir. At first the going was tough. The glory days of Tripura gymnastics had been forgotten and not too many paid attention to a young girl from the state. But I am a fast learner and I gradually got into the thick of it and soon everyone in the camp was on their toes as the young girl no one wanted to coach was threatening to break into the national team. Baba being an SAI coach was aware of the progress I was making. The Andamans is a very special holiday destination and Port Blair has a direct flight from Kolkata. A lot of his friends and colleagues in SAI used to visit there for their vacations and they would keep Baba informed about my progress. When I finally made the cut and was selected for the Indian team in 2009, he was extremely happy. He informed all of his colleagues and superiors and they too were overjoyed to hear of a brother officer's daughter making the Indian team. The regional director told him, "Dulal, she is no longer just your daughter, she is a daughter of SAI now too." Baba was extremely proud and he threw a party for all his colleagues in the Andamans.

Baba and Nandi sir come to see me compete at the 2010 Commonwealth Games in New Delhi.

Baba had never seen me compete and that opportunity came next year at the 2010 Commonwealth Games. He made plans with Nandi sir and both came to Delhi and saw me compete. Their presence was a great boost and I wish Nandi sir had been there with me during my competition as well. He fell victim to federation politics and camp intrigue in the build up to the Games. With my performance impressing many, sir had been called to the camp in Pune. But after spending two months there, he was asked to return to Agartala. I had been performing well under his guidance and the decision came as a huge shock to both of us. He even went and pleaded with the powers to reverse their decision as his presence could help me get a medal on the vault. He was curtly told that there would be no going back on it and to return immediately. I was extremely upset and cried a lot. Sir did not even tell me before leaving. He came up to my room but did not have the heart to enter, as he too was extremely emotional. It was a theme that would repeat itself again in the coming years.

THE PRODUNOVA: THE BUFFALO DEFIES DEATH

The 2010 Commonwealth Games (CWG) was truly spectacular. I was mesmerised to see the Games being organised at such a big scale. Ashish Kumar created history for Indian gymnastics by winning two medals at the games, a silver and a bronze. It was the first time Indian gymnastics had delivered at the global stage. We could proudly roam around the Athletes Village and be proud of our sport. Earlier we were looked upon as sportspersons on a joyride. I am not sure how many would have even known that an Indian gymnastics team existed prior to the Delhi Games. All around us everyone was winning medals; it was a coming-of-age moment for Indian sports, and Ashish bhaiya had put *us* on the national map. You cannot put a value on his contribution to Indian gymnastics. Everyone remembers the first, be it Ashish bhaiya or Abhinav Bindra, who a couple of years earlier had destroyed the cynicism surrounding Indian sports by winning that elusive individual Olympic gold. The momentum of that gold and the two bronze medals won by Sushil Kumar in wrestling and Vijender in boxing was carried over to the Delhi Games where India broke through the hundred-medal mark and finished second in the medal tally, behind Australia.

Ashish bhaiya deservedly took the spotlight with his two medals, one of them a silver in the men's vault. In the euphoria post that podium finish, not too many paid attention to another finalist in the vault competition. Yes, I too had reached the final in Delhi 2010. But we are a culture that celebrates only winners so I am not surprised that it is not remembered.

Now in international competitions for women's artistic gymnastics, the sequence is like this—vault, uneven bars, beam, and floor exercises. In India too, we follow the same sequence in every competition. In the 2010 CWG, we were performing in front of the home crowd. But I did not feel the pressure as such. I remember that when my turn came for the vault routine, I was not happy with the alignment. I had to put a lot of effort to keep the apparatus in alignment with my view and the run-up area. I had to make a few adjustments. In the vault, the rule is to perform one forward and one backward vault. My first vault was a 'Forward Handspring Straight Body Somersault'. In the final I ran well, my flight was nice, but while landing my left hand touched the ground. I lost my balance, lost a point in penalty, and missed the medal. For the backward movement, I had to perform the 'Tsukahara Straight Body Vault' as decided. This time there was no mistake but overall I lost a chance to become a medallist in the Delhi CWG 2010.

I still feel had Nandi sir been allowed to be with me in the competition arena I would have surely got a medal like Ashish bhaiya. The pain of missing out on a medal cannot be explained and I cried many times. It is natural for sportspersons to cry. We build ourselves up for months, hoping to attain peak performance at a certain time. When all that amounts to nothing you feel empty, there is a void. You want to move on but you just can't.

Defeats and setbacks also make you tougher. In 2010, the boys and many others in my team jeered at me. I heard one male gymnast taunt, *"Ye bhains hai aur iska coach gadha"* (She is a buffalo and her coach a donkey). Hurtful comments and taunts became a routine. But I smartened under their jabs. I often voiced my resolve to Nandi sir. "Sir, I have to win in the next Commonwealth Games in 2014." It was almost a prayerful cry. The target was set—it was a medal at the Glasgow Games four years from then on. It was uncharted territory, no Indian female gymnast had won a medal at multi-discipline games, but I *needed* to win. I needed to prove myself. That stubborn streak in me had taken over.

I was determined to perform in the 2014 CWG but did not know how, except to train myself under Nandi sir's guidance. I was more than willing to put any amount of hard work towards the target. Nandi sir, in fact, had already drawn a blueprint of my career that he revealed gradually. But he could prognosticate the future of my career because of my strong will and ability to work hard. He knew that I would do more than he wanted me to do.

Like me Nandi sir too was very inspired by Abhinav Bindra's gold at the Beijing Olympics. He wanted to see me at that stage, have the Olympian tag next to my name. That was his dream. In fact, in India, every player cherishes the dream of competing at the Olympic Games. Nandi sir would often say, "Dipa, you can become the first girl and the only one so far to reach the Olympics."

Practicing on the terrace of our new house after
the Delhi Commonwealth Games.

The dejection of the miss at the Delhi Games was my motivation. Try as hard as I could, I could not forget the taunts that had been directed towards me. Sport though gives you many opportunities to redeem yourself. And within a year the smirk had been wiped off the faces of those who had questioned my ability. In the 2011 National Games held in Ranchi in Jharkhand, I won five gold medals in the all-round and all other four events: vault, uneven bars, beam, and floor. I was the best in the country, but instead of gloating and rubbing it in I knew deep within that there was still a massive gap between the top-class international gymnasts and me.

An example of that came soon enough. I missed qualifying for the 2012 London Olympics. At that time I was not ready to perform at the international level. We as a team had miles to go. But those Olympics once again shattered stereotypes, like the one in Beijing four years ago.

The Olympic medals of Saina Nehwal and Mary Kom at London gave a boost to women power in sports. The whole country was inspired, and this feat certainly had an impact in the Indian gymnastics circuit as well. The record six Indian medallists in the London Olympics were celebrated all over the country, irrespective of class, caste, religion, or wealth. They became the pride of the nation.

Seeing the icons of Indian sport on the Olympic podium kept me on course for my dream as well. The burning ambition of winning at the 2014 Commonwealth Games drove us on. Before the 2014 Glasgow Commonwealth Games, Nandi sir used to watch a lot of gymnastics events on YouTube. I was strong in the vault and Nandi sir would always plan for better combinations of vault exercises for me. In the 2010 CWG, my frontal vault, the Forward Handspring Straight Body Somersault, considered to be a difficult vault, only had a maximum of five difficulty points. That implied that even a small mistake in the execution would ensure that I would be out of the podium in the tournament.

At that point of time, the Produnova was the vault with the highest difficulty, with seven points. The Produnova move consists of a front handspring off the vault, followed by two-and-a-half somersaults. Nandi sir saw it many times on YouTube, and we would later watch the move being performed by select few gymnasts. He was convinced that this could be the only route for me through which I could make a mark in the gymnastics world. It was the X-factor that I needed. One day in the stadium itself he asked me, "Dipa, will you do the Produnova in the next Commonwealth Games?" There were only five to six months left for the Games to begin in Glasgow. But I did not have a second thought. I have always had huge faith in him. I said, "Sir, I am even ready to jump from the second floor of a building." So, the coach and the athlete were mentally ready. That was the first test for the both of us. The first major hurdle was crossed.

Another big problem was that every time the team was announced for any international tour, Nandi sir's name was conspicuously missing. In fact, I still feel that it is a perpetual problem in Indian sports that unless and until one becomes an accomplished star, the process of acquiring even basic facilities becomes difficult. On the contrary, it should be the other way around, if at all.

I remember participating in tournaments without proper shoes. In fact, I remember once my tracksuit was torn and Nandi sir sew it and then also gave me another set of the suit. When some journalists asked about it, I told them the truth and it became a controversy for Indian sports. I got some ill-fitting costumes for the Olympics but my focus was my game, so I did not bother. Nandi sir would always take care of the small things. In fact, I sincerely believe that Indian coaches are in all cases not inferior to foreign coaches. In fact, they are one of the best in the world. But they need proper support. If they are given the best support, in time, they too can produce the best results.

Ahead of the CWG 2014, I was in a better frame of mind. My fitness levels were absolutely fine. I had speed. I had power. And most of all, I had the zeal and courage to perform. I felt enthusiastic and the vaulting table looked exciting. Fear never touched me while performing any difficult exercise in gymnastics. Among gymnasts, one's courage and hard work are the two most important differentiating factors. Besides, I have huge faith in my coach. Faith generates courage. So, I was ready to do any amount of hard work for the most difficult vault in gymnastics history—the Produnova.

This vault is named after a famous gymnast of Russia called Yelena Produnova. She first performed it in 1999. Everyone was pretty shell-shocked when she executed it; the very nature of the vault has led to it being nicknamed the 'vault of death'. But I never thought of it like that. Even Nandi sir detested this name. I knew of his concern but it never bothered me, even though it had been completed by only a few in the world. That became an additional incentive for me to be a part of an elite league. Yelena Produnova of Russia, Yamilet Pena of Dominican Republic, Fadwa Mahmoud of Egypt, and my hero Oksana Chusovitina of Uzbekistan were the only gymnasts who had completed this difficult but immensely beautiful vault in a competition.

In fact, I later learnt that Choe Jong Sill of North Korea was the first one to try a Handspring Double Front vault in the Moscow Olympics in 1980 but she could not land properly at that time. Proper landing is the most difficult aspect of this vault. No one had completed this up until the 19-year-old Yelena Produnova pulled it off and then had the honour of having the vault named after her. Ever since, this vault is known as the Produnova. Produnova used to do it with an élan which impressed the world and thus she set a milestone for generations to come. She accomplished this difficult vault in the 1999 World Championships in Tianjin in China.

A few months before CWG 2014, when both of us were ready, Nandi sir spoke to Mr Indrajit Singh Pabla, the project officer with the Sports Authority of India, about it. Mr Pabla, being a gymnast himself at one point of time in his career, understood the content of the message. He asked, "What do you want for this?" Nandi sir asked for a foam pit to practice the Produnova. Pabla sir somehow convinced the then director general of SAI, Mr Jiji Thomson. Within a month a foam pit costing between twenty-five to thirty lakh rupees was ready for us at the Indira Gandhi Indoor Stadium in Delhi.

Nandi sir is a hard taskmaster and I have to constantly follow a routine of exercises in the gymnasium.

The focus is on Tokyo 2020. My injury has robbed me of a year and a half of crucial training but I am determined to get back to my best soon.

No dream is small. You have to believe in yourself.

The Indira Gandhi Indoor Stadium in New Delhi has been my second home.

What have I achieved? Nothing barring a bronze medal at the 2014 Commonwealth Games. I have a long way to go. Rio has whetted my appetite. *Ye Dil Maange More!*

Gymnastics demands perfection every day and in every session. My injury at the beginning of 2017 was a huge setback but gradually I have worked my way back into contention. I still have a lot of catching up to do.

Gymnastics is a lonely sport. My parents have gotten used to my absence but there are times, especially during festivals, when you want to be home.

Vaulting has been my ticket to success at international competitions but my first love was the beam. My first gold medal too came on the beam at the North East Festival so many years ago.

The contact with the beat board is the most essential element during a vault. I am very finicky when it comes to the placing of the board as one misstep will cost me valuable points.

Vaulting is a complex discipline. You have to be spot-on for every single attempt. One slip-up and it can get very nasty.

This is not just my journey, it is our journey. Nandi sir has devoted more time to me than to his family. I had promised him a Dronacharya Award and thankfully my Rio performance saw him get the coveted award.

The Buffalo and the Donkey. As Sachin Tendulkar once said, we have turned the stones thrown at us into milestones.

Before practicing in the foam pit, Nandi sir asked me to run and do a double front on the floor itself, a basic floor exercise. I did this for a week. I was practising hard. It gave Nandi sir and myself huge amount of confidence. We would watch this vault on YouTube again and again. I would also watch Ashish bhaiya and another gymnast Mayank Srivastav performing the Produnova. After practising the vault for about two months in the foam pit, I was asked to do it on the mat. Gradually, I got the confidence needed to be able to perform it in international tournaments. I would fall but I never got hurt. There was no serious injury during the practice.

One problem was to get the approval of the chief coach Dr GS Bawa along with the consent of the team management. The fellow gymnasts would see me performing the vault during practice. So they were aware of it. But the Indian camp and the team management appeared to be divided over my practice and performing the Produnova vault. Later, I came to know that even the American coach Jim Holt was quite negative about the whole thing. Holt would tell everyone in the camp for the Commonwealth Games in New Delhi that Nandi sir was unnecessarily taking a high risk with me. Instead of talking to Nandi sir or me he kept telling the entire camp about it, which upset sir a lot.

When Nandi sir told Dr GS Bawa about my attempting the Produnova in the coming CWG, he responded, "Don't do it." He was scared. So, on the day of the trial Nandi sir stopped me from doing it before the team. There were only a few days left for the Glasgow CWG to begin. I cried a lot and fought with Nandi sir.

Nandi sir somehow convinced Dr Bawa later. The very next day I got a chance to show them my skill and the hard work we had put together. I performed the Produnova vault before the entire team, sweeping all apprehensions by my flawless performance coming from sheer hard work. The moment I landed, everybody started clapping. I took a huge sigh of relief. Nandi sir was in tears. The beauty, perfection, and the grind behind it, earned me the permission to do it in the Glasgow CWG. I passed the first test.

I was practising really hard for the coming CWG. Six to eight hours every day. I used to do eight to ten repetitions every day. We used to spend almost six hours for vaulting exercises and around two hours in conditioning exercises. It was not easy at all. In fact it was quite painful. Sometimes I used to cry a lot and complain to Nandi sir that I was not a machine. Sometimes, he used to allow me to rest. But then I used to cry and say, "I will keep doing it. I want to see how many times you can force me to do it again and again." We didn't have smooth times. He forced me to practice hard and I fought a lot. Before going to the Glasgow CWG I had done the Produnova around five or six hundred times and we were quite satisfied. I had attained a level of perfection on the classic Produnova vault.

As we reached Scotland, we wanted to start our practice session as soon as we could. But my start in Scotland proved to be a difficult one. In the qualification round, during the warm-up time itself, my ankle got hurt. But, I performed all the exercises with a hurt ankle, even the Produnova.

Nandi sir was really angry. He left all of us and went to his room. Later I was told that he cried a lot. His complaint was that my attempt for the Produnova itself was wrong. Besides, he was very disheartened. He thought that the Games were over for me before they had even started. He was also scared about what he would tell the authorities and the other members in the team. It had been a struggle for him to gain acceptance within the coaching set-up. He was the outsider and he sort of felt that with this defeat the walls would close on his coaching career in the national team.

Nandi sir is a very emotional man. Since he had locked himself up in his room and wasn't to be seen at the dining hall or within the Village there was no way for anyone to get in touch with him. I was hobbling around and was advised rest. Finally around one in the night some of my teammates decided that it was time to snap him out of his dark mood. He was staying on the second floor in another wing of the building the Indian team was put up in.

The girls shouted, "Nandi sir, Didi (Dipa) has qualified." That did it. He did not believe it. He came running to the ground floor to crosscheck whether it was a prank. They told him that I had come seventh in the qualification round and had reached the final. The transformation was immediate. Suddenly he was bouncing, more energetic and talking in an excited voice. I stayed away though. It may have been a weight off his shoulder but for me it was still a disaster. I had not performed anywhere close to my potential and was afraid of looking him in the eye. I waited for my teammates to return and on learning that sir had snapped out of his mood I too relaxed a bit and went off to sleep.

He came to meet me the next morning and immediately took me to meet the doctor in the Games Village. The doctor saw my swollen ankle and told me that it appeared to be a hairline fracture. He asked us to get an X-ray done and gave me some painkillers meanwhile. I took the painkillers and other medicines but I preferred to wrap my foot tightly with a crepe bandage than get an X-ray done. It was a peculiar situation. Here was I, on the cusp of achieving a dream that had dominated four years of my life and I was not sure whether I could even compete. The crushing defeat in Delhi and the taunts that I had endured had carried me through till this day. I did not want to finish out of the medals and face ridicule again. The anger and the stubbornness kicked in. Goodbye X-ray. To hell with it. I was willing to have my ankle in a cast for the next three months or even six months. You do hear of sportspersons digging deep and finding that little bit extra when they need it the most. This was when I needed to find that extra few per cent which would give me the strength to ignore the pain.

The final was to happen three days later on the 31st of July. I could not practice for another three days. But Nandi sir was still confident that I would do well. We did keep training, just enough to keep the body in shape. Nothing fancy, nothing hard that would cause the ankle more discomfort. I used to say that I would surely get a medal but sir would always ask me to keep mum. He always has been a very superstitious man. I had nothing to lose and I decided to go for it. The team knew I was injured, they just didn't know the fire raging within to not quit.

As I stood at the top of my mark on the day of the final, I just thought one thing. Keep it simple. Land the vault and ignore the pain. The first vault was going to be the most important one. It was the Tsukahara 360. If I could not land it then it was over as the Produnova would need a much bigger effort and there is only that much an injured ankle can take. I set off, eyes on the beat board and nothing else. There was no stopping me; momentarily the pain had gone and I hit the vault perfectly. The landing was not the best; I was not in control and I fleetingly stepped over the red line and was docked a 0.1 penalty as well. But importantly the ankle held up. As I walked back to the top of my mark I made eye contact with sir and gestured to fix the beat board for the next attempt. I glanced up at the large monitor to catch a replay and was very happy with the aggression I showed. The score soon flashed on the display board. Despite the not-so-great landing, I had scored a 13.633. I was way off the pace as far as the medal hunt was concerned. Later I realised it was the lowest score among all eight finalists on the first attempt.

To win a medal, I needed a big one. I knew I had the Produnova coming up. I felt good. The ankle was not hurting. Everyone else—the coaches, the finalists, and the judges—knew I was going to attempt it. It was a hit or miss moment; if I landed it, it would give me a lot of points. My other competitors had all decided to play safe. The highest difficulty level, attempted apart from me, was a 5.600 by England's Claudia Fragapane. The Produnova had a difficulty rating of 7.00.

The crowd too knew that this was going to be a difficult vault. As I stood at the top of my mark the whistles and the cheering gradually ceased. There was pin drop silence as I thundered down the mat. I had done this on a daily basis in

New Delhi. It was the easiest vault in the world. I knew it was mine. I knew this was in the bag.

I hit the beat board, got the elevation and landed on my feet. The crowd went wild. The emotions came pouring out. Usually I do not react much after a vault. Not that day, though. Within a second of landing I knew that I had just sent shockwaves throughout world gymnastics. A huge smile appeared on my face. I do not know what took over me; it was perhaps the release of the tension and the stress. That ankle be damned. It had done its job and held up. I punched the air in delight and ran down towards the athletes' area where sir waited with a huge grin on his face. As I came down he came towards me and hugged me. The other gymnasts sitting there quietly applauded; they know when they have seen something special and extraordinary. There was a Welsh coach standing a few feet from us and he took a few steps towards me with his fist raised. I did not need a second invitation and high-fived him. I turned around, the adrenaline still pumping. I looked towards the athletes' area in the stands where the Indian team was sitting. Some of my teammates had a look of disbelief. A few saw me waving and waved back.

A cameraman came over to us to get the reaction shot. I waved into the camera but after that both Nandi sir and I had eyes only for the large screen on top of the arena. It was a nervous wait as they showed the replay of the vault, giving me a chance to see it as well. All sorts of emotions flash through your mind. How much will they score it, will it be enough? Can it take me into a medal position? It is a nerve-wracking wait.

But as the wait went on, it also calmed me down. The euphoria was finally settling down and as I kept looking up, sir kept pacing up and down to see if the score was being declared in the athletes' area. After more than a minute they flashed it on the screens and on the monitor. It was a 15.100; I was the only gymnast to break through the 15-point barrier that day. As I processed that, it took me a few seconds to realise the other significant number that was flashing on the screen. The overall score was 14.366 after taking both the scores into account. And next to it flashed the position 2. I had gone from eighth place to second place with one vault. And then it dawned on me after a couple of seconds that I was behind Canada's Ellie Black and there was just one more gymnast left to compete, England's Claudia Fragapane. The medal was mine. I turned to sir and tried to high-five him telling him it was done. Sir was his usual self, being careful and not being in a rush to go overboard without reconfirming. A second later he too realised. We had done it. The medal was in the bag. A smile broke out and he leant forward and kissed me on the forehead. I looked up to the Indian team and blew flying kisses at them. The coaches, my teammates, and even Ashish bhaiya were on their feet cheering. These were very rare moments in our sport and everyone wanted to soak in as much as they could. It did not matter that in a few minutes I would come down to third with Fragapane landing her vault perfectly to take the gold medal. I had gone there to win a medal, I would be returning with a medal. The doctor had told me to pull out. I had become the first Indian woman to win a gymnastics medal.

The buffalo and the donkey had the last laugh. Thank you, Yelena Produnova.

In less than two months' time I went to the Asian Games in Incheon. But frankly speaking, I did not expect to return with a medal. Every sportsperson has a peak and a down phase. I had pushed myself really hard for a Commonwealth Games medal and knew that the competition in the Asian Games was very tough. Yet I finished fourth in the vault final. My score of 14.200 was a little lower than the CWG score. The other gymnasts, Hong Un-jong, Oksana Chusovitina, and Phan Thi Hai Thanh decorated the podium in the Incheon Asian Games. It hurt missing out on a medal but I was happy that I was not far behind the top three medallists. The Produnova was no longer an X-factor. It had changed the game for me.

FROM SLAP TO CLAP

Winning is everything in world sport. You win a medal, you are feted; you return empty-handed and no one is at the airport to receive you. I had gone through the entire gamut of emotions over the course of my career till the high of the medal at Glasgow. A part of me wanted to rebel, to shout from the rooftops, and call out everyone who had belittled me. I still do not understand why we wait for the first opportunity to pull someone down. The pursuit of sporting excellence is a long road, of course there will be bumps along the way but we do not seem to have the foresight to put a comforting arm around a sportsperson when he or she is reeling after a not-so-good performance. Trust me, it is then that we need the support. I am not going on a rant but thankfully Glasgow 2014 finally gave me the belief to walk into the subsequent national camp with a sense of purpose, with a sense of finally having achieved something for the country. I had been humiliated, faced ridicule, and been slapped as well over the years and finally I could break free from those traumatic memories.

The London World Championships in 2009 was my first international competition. It was the big stage and I was rather overawed and mesmerised by the occasion. I was naïve and had a 'boy-cut' hairstyle back then, the same one which had confused the passport authorities At times I would stop at the different apparatus to watch world-class gymnasts displaying their talent to the world. I was thoroughly impressed by big stars like Bridget Sloan and Rebecca Bross of the USA and Koko Tsurumi of Japan. I was a kid in a candy shop, no one to guide me or mentor me.

My fan moments also got me into big trouble. The focus was not there and it was affecting the rest of the squad. On one occasion, a didi (a senior Indian gymnast) got so angry with me that she scolded and slapped me twice or thrice right there, saying that I did not deserve to be at that competition. She berated me by saying that I should not have been given a chance to participate in a big tournament like the World Championships and that I should have rather participated in some smaller international tournaments first.

I was upset, yes, I would not and cannot deny it. But when you are young, you tend to get swayed by moments that are good and you push the painful memories away. I was never going to win a medal, in fact had I made the Top-100 it would have been considered an achievement. Now imagine my surprise when I received a huge cheer as I began my floor routine during the qualifying round. There were a few Indian fans at the famous O2 arena in London and they were on their feet, cheering for me even though I was not close to being perfect. Later someone told me that it was not me they were cheering for but the number on which I was performing. Bollywood is universal and my track for the routine was Madhuri Dixit's famous 'Ek do teen' from the movie *Tezaab*. Rather than feeling disheartened, I lapped up the attention. As far as I was concerned, for the rest of the spectators, a section of Indian fans were cheering for an Indian gymnast.

I had a better outing on the vaulting table when I did a handspring pike frontal vault and a straight body as my backward vault exercise. Now in gymnastics, the Tuck position or the 'closed body position' is considered to be the easiest one to perform while the 'straight body position' is the most difficult one. The Pike or 'semi-closed body position' is placed between these two. Nandi sir and I would always plan to perform the difficult exercises but it was a gradual learning process and we would never rush for any new thing. In fact, this is how the gymnastics world functions. It's always scientific and systematic. When I came back from the World Championships, I shared my experience of London with sir, which in turn helped us in planning for the events in the future.

Thankfully my fan girl moment at the World Championships did not cost me dearly. I was selected for the World School Games in Doha which was held two months after the World Championships. Travelling with Nandi sir to any international tournament was almost impossible at that point of time, as it was just my second international tournament. So I went there with Ruby ma'am from Uttar Pradesh as my coach. The World School Games were dominated by the Russian stars, specially Aliya Mustafina, who won four gold medals and also a silver in the tournament and mesmerised the entire gymnastics world. Aliya went on to show her class at the London Olympics in 2012 and also at the Rio Olympics in 2016. She won gold medals in uneven bars in London as well as at the Rio Olympics. I was rubbing shoulders with the best and every bit of the experience was helping me find my feet internationally.

We had a rather amusing incident on our return to India. Our camp was in Pune but our tickets were routed through New Delhi. The flight from Doha was late and we missed our connecting flight. Those of us who had to head back to Pune were stranded and had nowhere to go or anyone to fall back on as the rest of the team disembarked in New Delhi itself. We tried our best to reason with the airline officials but initially they too were reluctant to help. So with nothing to do we parked ourselves outside their counter hoping to know our fate soon. Finally after a wait of two hours they had pity on the young girls wearing Indian tracksuits and put us on a flight to Pune.

You can either be shaken by such incidents or mentally toughen up. I learnt from every incident and it fuelled my determination not to be cowed down. I do not know if it was rotten luck or just me but I seemed to attract trouble more often than not. My first international medal should have been a cause for much joy, but more than anything else it left a sour taste in the mouth. It started on an unpleasant note in the first place. We were informed about our participation at the Sultana Kamal Central South Asian Championships just three days before the competition and the selection happened on the basis of past performance. I had been in regular practice under Nandi sir and hence did not head to Dhaka undercooked. Surprisingly, sir was chosen to accompany the team for the competition which was held at the Mirpur Indoor Stadium in Dhaka. Infact the stadium is just about a kilometre from the Sher-E-Bangla National Cricket Stadium which Indian sports fans will connect with immediately.

My fellow teammates were Meenakshi from Punjab and Rucha Diwakar and Vandita Rawal from Maharashtra. We won the women's all-round event and I also won an individual gold in the vault, a silver each on the balancing beam and the individual all-round and a bronze medal in the uneven bars. My wait for an international medal was over; I would be returning with five! However I was not happy with the scores awarded to me as I felt I deserved to win the gold in the both the events where I was awarded the second position on the podium. That feeling of hurt was accentuated by an incident that left the entire team upset. Nandi sir was awarded a medal along with the team at the medal ceremony by virtue of being the coach. Now it is not usually the norm but in that tournament all coaches were felicitated. It was an unexpected joy and all of us were pretty chuffed that sir too had received a medal. Our joy was short-lived as a short while later he was asked to return the medal without any explanation. The coaches of the other teams on the podium, Bangladesh and Sri Lanka, were all wearing their medals but it came as a huge shock to the entire team that sir was asked to surrender his medal back to the organisers. Naturally we expected some kind of explanation but despite Dr GS Bawa being the tournament director, none was forthcoming. I had been witness to the repeated humiliations sir had to undergo over the years and this one was very hard to accept. I felt cheated. Sir tried to be casual about it but I could tell the pain he was going through. There was a small ceremony in Agartala when we returned home as the gymnastics fraternity celebrated our success but my heart wasn't in it at all.

There was pent up anger inside me. I felt we were being unfairly targeted. It wasn't just in the camp that was being held in New Delhi post the 2010 Commonwealth Games. The feeling of victimisation persisted even during our shopping trips to Pallika Bazar in Connaught Place.

While bargaining in the market, the smart shopkeepers would easily spot us to be non-native/outsiders. Our different accent in Hindi would always take the conversation in a different direction. The shopkeepers would often ask, "Where are you from?" I would go on to say, "Tripura", upon which the next query used to come quite often as, "Where is it? In Bangladesh?"

These expressions were very disheartening for both Nandi sir and me. I would always feel pity for their general knowledge about India. Tripura and other north-eastern states have always been marginalised in terms of sports and because of this, I wished that at least the people recognise it to be a part of the county's mainland.

During these times while shopping and sometimes also in some formal gathering, some would venture a guess as to whether I was a boxer or a wrestler. Often my biceps and sturdy built would confuse them. They would ask, "What do you do?"

"I am an athlete."

"What do you play? Are you into boxing or wrestling?"

"No," I would try to evade.

"I think, I have seen you wrestling," one would lie in typical Delhi bluster.

"No, I am a gymnast."

"So, you work in some circus. Do you do trapeze also?"

"It's not a circus. It's gymnastics and girls also do gymnastics," I would reply.

It hurt. It always did and it does even today.

I must reveal an interesting conversation that took place after my medal at the Commonwealth Games. We were still at the venue, long after the medal ceremony had ended. The team was together and the phones were ringing non-stop. I did notice sir talking animatedly to someone from a distance. It had been an emotional moment for him and his faith in me had been vindicated. The tears of joy are difficult to stop at times like this and all of us were content letting him be, even the other coaches who had always sneered at him. After a while he sought me out in that crowd and motioned me over. He handed the phone to me and I presumed it was someone from Tripura wanting to congratulate me. It turned out to be a former gymnast, the same one who had slapped me at my first international competition five years ago. She said, "I feel sorry I slapped you in your first international competition. I want to clap for you now. God bless." I said, "*Dhannobad.* Thank you so much," as tears rolled over my cheeks. This was the loudest clap for me. Life had come full circle.

THE ROAD TO RIO

The struggle of a sportsperson is never ending. It is a constant battle to prove your credentials. Breaking through in Indian sports is, especially, a tough ask. However, once you break through, all roadblocks seem to disappear.

One medal at the Commonwealth Games changed everything for me. We returned triumphant to Agartala. My foot was still in a sort of protective cast but the pain vanished as soon as I landed and met my parents at the airport. My medal had put Tripura on the sporting map of India once again and like the gymnasts of old, I too was put on top of an open jeep and paraded through the city. I was a bit overwhelmed, but for Nandi sir this was the dream of a lifetime. Many years ago he too had been inspired by a similar parade, one which had instilled in him the passion to become a gymnast. Hopefully that day in August a few more children got their inspiration to follow in my footsteps.

I spent two weeks at home, two memorable weeks where I hardly practiced despite the Asian Games not too far away. Since we could not risk surgery, we had decided to pursue a course in alternate medicine. I consulted an Ayurveda specialist and waited for the injury to naturally heal, but I knew there was no way I was going to be a hundred per cent fit for the Games which were being held in Incheon, South Korea.

There were not even two months between the Commonwealth and the Asian Games and I landed in Incheon not knowing if I could compete. But I have never been the one to shy away from a challenge and despite the injury, I qualified for the final of the vault. Sport has a way of putting you in your place and I finished fourth, yes just out of the medal bracket. It is ironic how a fourth place finish has hounded me through my career. I knew I was nowhere near my best but it was possible for me to return with a medal. I made a mistake that was extremely amateurish and my hand hit the mat on landing which saw me being hit with a penalty. I kept up a brave face all through the medal ceremony as I saw the national flags of the three gymnasts go up. But eventually I could not hold back and the tears started to flow. I knew I was capable of winning a medal. I could have pulled out of the competition but I had the belief that I was very much capable of landing myself on the podium.

Funny how sport can give you completely different emotions within a space of a few months. Two months previously I was flying high as I flew back from the Commonwealth Games and here I was returning home empty-handed. It did not matter that I was injured; no one remembers what shape you were on the day of your competition. All they remember is your eventual position. And in India if you do not win a medal at the Games then you have failed. There was a felicitation ceremony for medal winners at the Ashoka Hotel in New Delhi. Naturally I wasn't invited. There had been a similar ceremony after the Commonwealth Games and Bharat Ratna Sachin Tendulkar had been the chief guest. He had handed us cheques for the prize money that we were entitled to but surprisingly there had been no acknowledgement of my coach. He had been there in the audience, clapping and beaming as I had gone on stage, but there had been nothing for him. I just do not understand why we ignore our coaches during these happy times. It is their struggle and their commitment over a considerable period of time that sees a sportsperson stand on the podium.

I knew the sniggers would return when I joined the camp again; Nandi sir and I would face those taunts once more. But I realised that those taunts actually strengthened my resolve, they made me more determined. I once read that there were some batsmen the Australian cricket team would never sledge as they knew it could boomerang on them. I did not look tough but by then I had had enough and knew that there was just one way of shutting people up. On the mat.

There was no break after the Asian Games. The World Championships in 2014 were less than a month away and I had to forget the heartbreak and deliver a performance that would show that Glasgow was no fluke. But it all got a bit too much for sir. Everyday after the practice session all the campers would be lined up and the coaches would only praise the male gymnasts. It was as if we did not exist. Occasionally there would be a small word here and there to ensure we too were accommodated but while we didn't feel the discrimination as much, sir would be extremely upset. He wanted to change the perception and he felt that the taunts were mostly directed towards him. He would take out the frustration on us; since he worked mostly with the girls he would make us do extra sessions and exercises on his watch. One day though he called all of us together after practice and broke down. "They are saying that the girls cannot win anything, that they will win an occasional medal here and there but that is it," he muttered as he kept sobbing. He issued an ultimatum then. "I will leave the camp and never return if you do not start winning. I have staked my entire reputation on you and it is time now for you to repay my patience," he said that day.

Naturally we were all pretty upset to see him that emotional and we kept discussing his words over the next couple of days. Redemption came soon enough. The World Championships in Nanjing, China, saw me finish tenth. I was on standby for the final and it was a massive high. It was the first time that any Indian gymnast had reached this position and everyone in the team who was present at the tournament congratulated us. I looked at sir and he seemed pretty relieved. I would have been extremely happy had I reached the final but then considering that I was just about feeling my way back from a fracture, I could not complain much. More so considering that my performance had shut everyone up once and for all, there could be no excuses this time. This was the pinnacle of our sport and I had made my mark there, amongst the best gymnasts in the world. Sir was pretty relieved that my injury troubles were behind us and we could now start preparing in right earnest for a shot at qualifying for the 2016 Olympics in the following season. I had returned to the stage where I had once been a gawky teenager and held my ground against the likes of Simone Biles, Hong Un-jong and the rest. The belief was flowing through my mind that I was now ready for the big stage.

We threw ourselves completely into the preparations for the 2015 World Championships. The omens were good; it was to be held in Glasgow and in the same arena where I had won my medal at the Games a year ago. When you look back and scan the newspapers you won't find much written about Nandi sir or me. We both knew that we were knocking on the door. Life became a set routine. There was practice in the morning, then rest, and then practice in the evening. Holidays would be spent mostly in the hostel or perhaps the odd trip out to a mall in Delhi to watch a movie or to indulge in some shopping. Sir would always be there. He was our guardian angel. Not once would we be allowed to slip away from his gaze. He was extremely protective and kept us on a tight leash.

Perhaps the only distraction that year was in the months before the World Championships. The selection committee for the National Sports Awards recommended my name for the Arjuna Award. I was told that there was hardly any discussion on my name and I was one of the first names selected by the committee for the honour. It was a rare feat, both for my sport and for my state. Ashish bhaiya had won the Arjuna Award a few years earlier and I became the next gymnast to get it. It also ended a long wait for Tripura. Mantu Debnath and Kalpana Debnath were the other two gymnasts from the state to have received the award.

It was an extremely emotional moment for Nandi sir when he called to inform me about the award. It remained a regret all through his playing career that he was never considered for the award despite his achievements. Many players who were not as deserving and did not have the achievements which he possessed had received the award. Sir did not have a godfather, neither was he one to lobby for such awards. He moved on but kept the hurt within. He had once confessed to me that it had been one of his goals to receive an award from the President of India at the Rashtrapati Bhawan.

I was completely flattered by the pageantry and spectacle of the entire function. Protocol demanded that we undergo a dress rehearsal a day before the ceremony at Rashtrapati Bhawan and we also had to check into the Ashoka Hotel where all the winners were staying. It had been a good performance by India at both the Commonwealth Games and Asian Games in 2014 and there were a lot of familiar faces who were to receive the award along with me. Tennis star Sania Mirza was the recipient of the Rajiv Gandhi Khel Ratna, India's highest sporting honour. My fellow Arjuna awardees included hockey goalkeeper PR Sreejesh, shuttler Kidambi Srikanth, wrestlers Babita Phogat and Bajrang, and shooter Jitu Rai among others.

I cannot describe the feeling of standing in front of the President and waiting as your achievements are read out. Compared to the others who had been around for years and had won multiple medals for the country I felt a bit intimidated. Then there was also the nagging thought at the back of my mind of not tripping over and making a fool of myself. All the female awardees had to wear a saree along with a blazer. Most of us that day were not used to wearing a saree. We usually wear T-shirts and track pants through the day when not in practice. Who has the time to wear a saree! I did know how to drape one, and since it was not something I was used to I did struggle. And I also committed a major fashion faux pas, one that went largely unnoticed apart from one keenly observant eye on television.

Sir had accompanied me for the function and I wanted to acknowledge his role in getting me this honour. Obviously I could not breach protocol and get him to accept the award with me. I decided that I would take a part of him with me when I went up to receive my award. I walked into his room one day and demanded a pair of white socks. Naturally he was extremely taken aback and inquired why I needed a pair of male white socks. I explained my intention to him and ultimately bulldozed all objections and forced him to give me a pair. I wore those socks to the function and sir's wife, Soma madam, could make out I was wearing his socks as she watched the function on TV. She called him after the function asking why was I wearing socks, that too his, underneath my saree. He had no answer and said he was bullied into it, which was the truth.

After the awards, once President Pranab Mukherjee had left, I immediately sought sir out and handed him the award. "Sir, this is your award. Today I am giving you my Arjuna Award, next I will ensure that you get the Dronacharya Award and realise your dream of receiving an award from the President of India," I said to him. He fought back tears and told me that from now on there was no looking back and together we would achieve a lot more.

We had to return to Agartala for a small period as our then Chief Minister Mr Manik Sarkar wanted to felicitate me. I was promoted as a sports officer with the Sports Council but the bigger recognition was for Nandi sir. CM Sarkar announced the promotion of Nandi sir to the post of assistant director with the Sports Council. He had been ignored in New Delhi, but his state finally granted him the recognition he so richly deserved.

From Tripura to New Delhi and Glasgow and Incheon, it had been a memorable journey. It had been full of hardships and unexpected twists and turns and there was still more to come. Looking back, I feel it is these tough moments that have forged in me strength to withstand shocks and bash on regardless. The World Championships ended up being a bittersweet moment for the both of us. We had trained extremely hard for it and I was ready. I knew the gymnasts I was up against, not much had changed in the last year, but this time I was focussed and was not worried about my ankle as well. The vault was my best chance and I knew that I had a long way to go in the all-round event. The vault did not let me down. I qualified in seventh place for the final. It was the first time an Indian gymnast had reached the final at the World Championships. There were many stunned faces in the crowd that day in Glasgow. It mirrored the Olympics a year later. At least my fellow gymnasts knew all about me at Rio, this was an unexpected feat. An Indian in World Championships final! I was not surprised, neither was sir. An entire year had been devoted to getting here. A year ago I had finished tenth and was a standby for the final. This time I was in the final and would not have to endure a nervous wait to see if anyone dropped out.

Part one was done, part two was the more difficult bit. To earn a ticket to the Olympic Games in Rio de Janeiro I would have to win a medal. Now that was really expecting too much, wasn't it? Here I was, the first Indian in a World Championships final and that in itself was something to be extremely proud of. But I knew within that with my all-round scores being low I had to max my performance in the vault final or sit at home and watch the Olympics on television.

The Produnova did not let me down and I started the final with a strong vault. My second vault though saw me docked 0.300 as a penalty and I finished fifth, the best finish ever by an Indian at the World Championships. Those penalty points actually cost me a potential fourth place. But in the end, when the euphoria subsided, the truth hit me in the face. Goodbye, Olympics. I had not won a medal and with just the medallists earning individual quotas for Rio my chances were as good as over. There was slim chance that I could get a call-up for the test event at the Olympic venue in 2016 but those were dashed the same evening. The final rankings saw me at twenty-seventh place with twenty-four invited to the test event. My dreams were done; they had soared high on the vault and come crashing down. Nandi sir was left shaking his head at what had just transpired. "Dipa, your luck is out," he said emotionally. I burst into tears. It is difficult to explain the moment when you think your dreams are on the verge of being achieved and then in a flash they disappear. There was a void. We both felt empty. I had been a standby at the previous World Championships and did not get a chance to compete in the final. How would I now go past two others to keep my Olympic dream alive?

It was a subdued return to India. Of course everyone around me was extremely positive and kept congratulating me on my performance. But they didn't get the turmoil within. Coming fifth at World Championships was great, I got that. But I wanted to be an Olympian and all I could do was pray for a miracle.

Now even though on paper we didn't 'technically' have a chance, Nandi sir kept the training going. We trained daily in Agartala, away from the spotlight, hoping for an email or a phone call that we knew would not come. I have to credit sir for not giving up. He ensured I remained focussed and sharp. No other Indian gymnast had qualified so there was no national camp in Delhi. We were on our own.

Perhaps it was destined that my Olympic dream would stay alive. We had given up hope but with less than a month to go, the call came. For a variety of reasons three gymnasts had opted out. The miracle had unfolded; I was asked if I would make it to Rio for the Olympic test event. Imagine the panic that set in. We had under a month to prepare, get the logistics sorted, and also mentally get ready for a competition that had suddenly materialised. Our gymnastics federation could not help us as it had been suspended by the sports ministry. Nandi sir turned to the one man he knew who could make the impossible happen.

The project officer at the Sports Authority of India, Mr Pabla, once again rose to the occasion. He realised the urgency of the situation and immediately got a proposal up and running. He briefed the then director general of SAI, Mr Injeti Srinivas, and the proposal was cleared in an instant. I really have to appreciate the role of these two fine officers, for the speed at which things unfolded was unusually rapid by SAI standards. A camp was immediately sanctioned; I flew down to Delhi with sir. Obviously I couldn't practice alone and other gymnasts received urgent summons to report for the camp. Mr Pabla was tasked by Mr Srinivas with looking after the logistics and being a gymnast himself, he knew what had to be done. In fact he accompanied us to Rio for the test event.

The 2016 Olympiad was still a few months away when I landed in Rio for the test event. I may have been one of the first Indian sportspersons to get a first-hand experience of what was to follow. The Indian shooting team was also present around the same time for the World Cup but the distances were massive and I did not end up meeting them. There is a reason why pre-Olympic events are called test events. For us it was a matter of achieving our dreams and like me there were many other gymnasts who came to Rio, hoping to seal a ticket for the Rio Olympics. The city didn't look like it was hosting an Olympics in a few months, to be honest. Our competition venue was ready but there were logistical problems. Better still to have these problems before the Olympics than during it when the entire world is watching. I for one wasn't fazed when there was a power outage during the competition; we had it in Tripura all the time. For the other gymnasts it may have come as a rude shock.

Contrary to public perception, my qualification for the Olympics was not linked to my performance in the vault. That rule stood only for the World Championships. To qualify for the Olympics I had to get high scores in the women's all-round competition, which meant I had to be solid on the four apparatus: the vault, the uneven bars, the beam and finally the floor. The all-round is the basis for qualification for the individual events as well and the top eight performers in each apparatus go through to the final. To ensure a level-playing field, gymnasts from the countries that were entered in the team competition could not qualify from the all-round competition. Since only four teams were guaranteed Olympic berths, it meant the gymnasts from the remaining teams would have to be content with just one berth if they topped the all-round standings.

That rule played into my hands; I was confident that if a few big names were ineligible then I could easily sail through. The Swiss gymnast, Giulia Steingruber, topped the all-round charts but could not take her team through to the qualifying berth. As a result she took the lone qualifying spot for her country for the Olympics. Qualification done, she did not compete in the final of the two individual events. Steingruber jointly topped the vault qualification along with me; we both had a combined score of 15.166 after our two attempts. That put me in the final of the vault but the job was still not done. I had to hold it together in the other three apparatus as well. I was not spectacular but I did enough to finish forty second in the overall standings. It didn't look very great but when you removed the gymnasts who were ineligible or had bagged a lone qualifying spot, I was ranked tenth. I had booked my ticket to the Olympic Games. At the end of a long day, when the scores were finally compiled after all the four sub-divisions had finished their routines, Nandi sir and I could finally smile. I was excited and naturally so, I had become the first Indian woman to qualify for the Olympic Games. But the celebrations were muted. Nandi sir had got wind that Steingruber would not be competing in the final of the vault the next day. An opportunity presented itself of winning a gold medal at a world-level competition for the first time. Since we didn't have much time, we celebrated with a quiet dinner and then it was off to bed to ensure I was completely ready for the final the next day.

My idol, Oksana, had also qualified for the vault final. She had clinched her Olympic spot with me the day before and I was extremely excited to compete against a gymnast who has been an all-time legend of the sport. Sir and I had decided that we would not deviate from the plan that had worked so well for us on this short trip. I started the final with the Produnova. It was a decent landing, not my best, and saw me get an execution score of 8.100 which meant I had scored 15.100 which was the best for the first series amongst the eight finalists. The execution score was the lowest of the eight finalists but the difficulty score of the Produnova is 7.00 and that took me into the lead. I knew I had the gold medal in my sights, I just had to ensure there were no mistakes as I thundered down the runway for my second attempt. The pressure of qualifying was off; I knew that irrespective of the result my berth for the Olympics had been sealed. I hit the board, executed my vault to perfection and landed on the mat. After a while the score flashed on the screen, it was a 14.566, which meant I had won the gold ahead of Oksana. I rushed into sir's arms as we both hugged each other. We both turned to wave to Mr Pabla who was jumping up and down in the stands.

I have stood on victory podiums before, won medals in international competitions as well, but this one was extremely special. I am not sure if the national anthem has ever played before in Brazil at a sporting event, well it definitely had never played before at a gymnastics event, that too a world-level tournament. As I saw the tri-colour going up during the victory ceremony, I knew that I could repeat this feat in a few months from now. My progression through the ranks had been gradual, I had been a finalist at the World Championships and now I was a gold medallist.

By this time Pabla sir had informed his superiors of the result and as evening approached, his phone started to ring non-stop. None of us had taken a local number but we were connected to the internet at the hotel where we were staying and courtesy WhatsApp the phones kept ringing. I spoke to my parents, also to Mr Srinivas and thanked him for all his support. He assured me that by the time I returned to New Delhi, the plan for the Olympics would be sanctioned and put into place. I knew then that I was not going to go home for a while. Nandi sir too told Soma madam the same.

The next morning Nandi sir and Mr Pabla sat down, discussed what was needed for the next three months and Mr Pabla sent it to his office in New Delhi. I was happy, knowing that I would return to this city in a few months as I packed for our return journey.

Till then I had not realised what this success meant. But the euphoria which the gold medal had generated became obvious when I landed in New Delhi after a really long flight. I really wanted to get to the hostel at the Indira Gandhi Stadium and crash. We were received by SAI officials and were tipped off that there was a huge media contingent waiting outside. We were told we had to get to the SAI office to meet Mr Srinivas in a few hours while Nandi sir received a few calls from the federation informing him of a press conference around the same time. I was rather taken aback by the scrum among the assembled media for photos, a quote, or an interview for the television cameras. In that melee you can't distinguish between anyone and I was just hoping to be whisked away so that I could sleep for a while.

Sleep, though, was impossible as the phones kept buzzing. Parents, family, friends, campers, well-wishers, everyone kept calling. It is par for course when you win I guess, I had hardly seen any media covering my training during the days I was in New Delhi, barring a few familiar faces. That day was an extremely long one. Sir and I were felicitated by Mr Srinivas and he assured us of all support for the Olympics. "Go abroad and train if you want to, no expense will be spared," were his words. Friends in the media were there too and this time there was no avoiding them. I was later told that most of them were waiting for me at a hotel near the airport at the press conference organised by the federation. We had received no support from the federation over the last month, yet here they were celebrating my success. Mr Srinivas bundled us off to the hostel and told us to get some rest, as training for the Olympics was now about to begin.

The next few days were a blur. There seemed a steady procession of journalists who wanted to talk to me, know my story, and report on a rare high for Indian sport in a truly global sport. Jet lag was an issue but you know Nandi sir, practice for him is non-negotiable. The administrator of the stadium, Ms Manjushree Dayanand, stepped in here and ensured that there would be no disturbances during training. Of course it made her very unpopular with the media but both Nandi sir and I needed to move on. Most of my competitors had already qualified at the World Championships and were beginning their final preparations to peak at Rio. We, on the other hand, were playing catch up and were way behind the pace.

True to his word, Mr Srinivas ensured the import of the best gymnastic equipment available in next to no time. I do not know how procurement procedures, which end up taking months, were bypassed, but by the time I began my final preparations for the Olympics, I was training on world-class equipment. Nandi sir and I decided that we would not go abroad, everything we needed was here in New Delhi and there was no point heading to an alien environment with barely months left for the Olympics.

Time was not on our side, we both knew it. We decided to cut out any distractions, as even a day's loss could not be made up. This is where sir's dedication and commitment came through. One day he received a phone call from the secretary of Bharat Ratna Sachin Tendulkar. Tendulkar sir had accepted the invitation of the Indian Olympic Association to become an ambassador for the Indian contingent and wanted to personally meet the sportspersons who were heading to Rio. My triumph had been splashed all over the media and he was keen to meet me and share his vast knowledge with me. It was an offer few would refuse. But Nandi sir was not impressed. He stressed the importance of my training sessions to Tendulkar sir's staff and told them there was no way he would allow me to miss training. The staff tried their best to convince him; they said they would send a car to ensure that we both were comfortable, but sir was adamant. He understood the gesture but it was not possible for us to head over to where Sachin Tendulkar was to meet the other Rio-bound players. His staff pleaded and tried to change his mind but to no avail. Sir was steadfast and even though I was very keen to meet one of the most iconic sportspersons of the country, I knew sir was right. Later we did meet Tendulkar sir when he came to the Athletes Village in Rio, the day after the opening ceremony.

Nandi sir was pleasantly surprised when Tendulkar sir remarked that he was a very focussed coach when they were introduced. Obviously his team would have told him the reasons for my no show and Sachin Tendulkar being a sportsperson first and foremost had recognised the commitment to training which is what we all aspire to achieve daily.

FOUR-FOOT SOMETHING

Sometimes the most well-laid plans can be turned upside down in a jiffy. Our no-distractions policy met a similar fate, just days ahead of my departure for Rio. I had just finished a morning training session when Nandi sir informed me that we had to head over to a hotel in South Delhi for the official send-off ceremony organised by the Indian Olympic Association.

Now, Nandi sir is a stickler for punctuality, or rather he hates being late, so as was wont to happen we reached the venue much before the other sportspersons arrived. I gathered that most of the Rio-bound squad would be there so I was looking forward to interacting with a few. Nandi sir had made it clear that I would not speak to the media without him being present so I wandered off into the hall where the function was to be held and sat down on the seats reserved for the Olympic team.

One by one they started arriving. I saw wrestlers Vinesh Phogat and Babita Phogat and we acknowledged each other, having been teammates at the 2014 Commonwealth Games. As more and more players arrived it struck me that we all belonged to a very elite club. We had all represented India at major events, the World Championships of our various sports or the Asiad or the Commonwealth Games. Yet we had been chosen by our federation to represent the country and our sport for those events. At the Olympics it was completely different. Every one of those sportspersons at the ceremony had qualified on his or her merit. Some like me had come through a tough qualifying tournament, some like the badminton players had qualified on the basis of their world rankings, a result of some consistent performances over the last twelve months. It was at that moment that the enormity of my achievement actually hit me. A few days earlier the accreditation card for the Olympics had arrived. I had been curious to see it but that was about it. It hadn't given me goose bumps or caused me to break into a jig. In fact Nandi sir had been more worried that I would misplace it and end up not going to Rio, as that accreditation card also doubled up as a visa. Such had been his paranoia that I had told him to keep the cards. Along with the card he had also received the ceremonial kit for the games from the IOA office. You could see the emotion on his face as he proudly tried out the blazer with the words Rio Olympic Games emblazoned on the left pocket alongside the Indian Olympic Association logo. We used to receive one for each Games we attended but the Olympic blazer was the one which was the most coveted one.

I was quite surprised to be called to officially unveil the team kit for the Games. The other sportspersons invited on stage, 2012 Olympic medallists Saina Nehwal and Yogeshwar Dutt, had not arrived so I ended up doing the honours instead. The master of ceremonies referred to me as four-foot something I didn't take offence to it even though a few people present there came up to me and said it bordered on disrespectful. I didn't care. Till then I had not realised the nature of my success; I had always felt that I had done nothing compared to the legends with whom I was to share the stage. I was in dreamland and the afternoon was about to get better. As I sat and waited for the felicitations to begin, I saw a flurry of activity to my left. Naturally I looked that way to know what was the reason for the sudden activity as one of the IOA office bearers was speaking on stage. To my utter amazement I realised that standing there was Bollywood actor Salman Khan and next to him was music maestro AR Rahman. Both had accepted the IOA's invitation to be ambassadors for the Olympic team and were there in that capacity. It seems their presence at the function was known to most but I had absolutely no idea as I was living largely in a cocoon. I immediately turned to sir and said, "See, Salman Khan is standing there!" Imagine my surprise when he replied that he knew about it.

Both Khan and Rahman personally wished each of the Olympians the best on stage and when my name was read, I too went on stage. That for me was enough. As the function went on, I slipped out of the hall and immediately called up Puja. My sister is a huge fan of Khan and she just could not believe that her favourite actor had 'officially' sent me on my way to Rio! The afternoon could have been even more memorable had Nandi sir relaxed his rules a bit. After lunch all the Rio-bound sportspersons were invited to Mr Khan's room for a photo session. I badly wanted to go but sir refused, as we had to be back at the camp for the evening training session. So back I went to the stadium, changed into my costume, and was on the mat at exactly the right time. There was no time for rest; it did not matter that it had been a long day, there was no escaping a session a few days before the Olympics!

There was a bigger surprise in store a few days later. Go Sports Foundation, who had funded a part of my training, flew down my parents a few days before my departure for Rio. I was meeting Baba after a gap of nearly eighteen months and Ma after three months, since I had come to New Delhi to prepare for the test event. In all these years it was the first time Ma saw me training; I had never allowed her to enter the Byamagar or the NSRCC back in Agartala and all she had seen was my performances on television. Baba had come to see me compete at the 2010 Commonwealth Games. My parents never admit it but they miss me a lot. However a lifetime spent in sport has conditioned both them and us two sisters.

The farewells didn't end there. All the campers at the hostel gathered together the night I was leaving for Rio. A cake was cut and there were smiles all around as everyone was in high spirits. I was off to make history for our sport and everyone had played their part over the last three months to get me ready for Rio. There was no reason for them to come every day and sweat it out in the gym. They weren't going to Rio and neither were the other coaches going to accompany Nandi sir and me. Yet there was a spirit of togetherness and it didn't end there. Almost all of them accompanied me to the airport that night as well. My physio Sajad Ahmed Mir was to undertake the journey twice. He was to fly out the next day to join us in Rio but even he came along to the airport. Our Chief Coach Bawa sir was there too and lots of photos were clicked outside the international terminal. My friend Aruna Reddy was flying home to Hyderabad the next morning and we had planned it in such a way that we would be together at the airport till I left and then she would head over to the domestic departures section. So waving a final goodbye, Aruna, sir, and I entered the airport. But the see-off party didn't leave. They kept waiting for us and only after Nandi sir called two hours later saying we had cleared immigration and were waiting at the gate did they return back to the stadium.

Our flight was to depart at four in the morning; it was an Etihad airways flight with a stopover in Abu Dhabi. Nandi sir, being his usual self, kept hustling to leave as early as possible despite my protests so we reached the airport at around half past twelve and even after clearing immigration had a lot of time on our hands.

I was naïve enough to think that Aruna would join me in the departures section after the security check. We both had made grand plans of window shopping to kill time. It was only after I crossed immigration and called her did I realise that she was in a different part of the airport. She was in the domestic departures while I was in the international departures section. It was pretty foolish of the both of us and my biggest regret was that I had not even said bye to her. Nothing could be done now and we both said our goodbyes on the phone.

I always make it a point to have a burger at McDonalds when I am at the New Delhi airport. This time too my eyes immediately went towards the first floor where the food court is located. Nandi sir knew about my habits and he immediately put an end to it, saying no junk food this time. There was no point arguing with him and I snuck sneaky glances towards the McDonalds outlet as we walked towards the departure gates. I called my parents, who were up, one last time, telling them I had checked in and they could go to sleep. As always Ma gave me her parting advice. She told me not to be nervous the day of the competition. "You do not do well when you are tensed, avoid it. Remember the Asian Games, you looked nervous and that is why you committed a mistake when your hand hit the floor while landing," she said. Mothers always know, even mine who had never been to a competition ever. Baba was his usual relaxed self, he told me to go step by step and aim for reaching the finals first before thinking of anything else.

It had been a long day and I was extremely tired and sleepy. We had had training sessions both in the morning and in the evening and now there was a lengthy wait till the flight took off. I found a chair and comfortably curled up—the advantage of being four-foot something. I knew Nandi sir would be the alarm clock; there was no way he was going to sleep till the flight actually took off. He woke me up when the boarding started and I have vague memories of stumbling into the flight and dropping off to sleep again. We had not even left the parking bay but my eyes were burning and I didn't need anyone's permission.

Sir woke me up after a few hours as breakfast was being served. The flight from Delhi to Abu Dhabi is not a very long one, under four hours to be exact. I am not a fan of aircraft food so I drank a cup of coffee and opened my bag which had a few biscuit packets as well a packet of *chura bhaja* or flattened rice. Thankfully we didn't have to walk too much while changing planes in Abu Dhabi; I was tired to the point of exhaustion and so was sir. We boarded our connecting flight without any trouble but were dismayed to note that our seats for the really long journey to Rio were bang in the middle of the middle row. We would have preferred the aisle seats but here we were, at the mercy of two other passengers if we even wanted to get up for anything. Anyway, that was a problem that would be sorted out later. For now, I wanted to get back to sleep.

As soon as the plane took off I told sir that I could not sleep in the sitting position. My body was terribly aching after that short flight from New Delhi and I needed to stretch my legs. I told him I was going to sleep on the floor. I wish I had clicked a photo of his incredulous face when I made that statement. I was wearing an India T-shirt and probably could pass of for a small kid. Sir was having none of it. "You are going to the Olympics! What will people say?" "I do not care what people think, sir. I need to sleep properly or will have a stiff neck when we land in Rio." I did not want to risk getting a yelling on the plane so I quietly curled up in my chair and dropped off to sleep. Sir later told me that within half an hour my leg had crossed over the seat rest and come to rest on the knees of the gentlemen who was on the seat next to me. Sir was pretty embarrassed and kept profusely apologising to the poor passenger who was quite elderly. He tried to wake me up but the good Samaritan said he had no problem and did not let sir wake me up. Sir was too exhausted himself and managed a few hours of sleep. By this time I had changed my position and the leg had gone in the other direction, on to sir's side. He woke up and then spent the next two hours walking up and down the aisle while I slept like a baby. He did take a few photos and showed it to me when I finally woke up, knowing I would not believe him.

Fifteen hours on an economy ticket is no laughing matter. But we got there finally. It was my second trip in four months and I was not too excited. I had heard a lot about the Olympic atmosphere in a host city while at the test event but this time too I was disappointed. I felt as if I had landed in any other city in the world and not the host city of the Olympics, which were to get underway in a week. There was a separate queue for the Olympic athletes and we cleared immigration pretty quickly and found ourselves on a bus headed to the Games Village. The ride was a long one and the seats were much more comfortable than the ones on the aircraft and I once again dozed off.

There were a few formalities that had to be completed when we arrived at the Athletes Village. I had prior experience of Athletes Villages and this one felt no different initially. But within a few minutes we knew that it was very different. For starters it was massive. We needed a shuttle to take us to our quarters but as luck would have it, we got lost. The administrative staff had told us that the Indian team was staying in Tower 29, right next to the building housing the Brazilian delegation. That should have been good enough except that we didn't know where to get off. We kept looking out of the windows to spot the Brazilian building but it was dark and we could not. So we ended getting a full tour of the Village as the bus made its scheduled stops at the dining hall, the international zone, and the transport mall. By then we had realised that we were back where we had started, since even the driver could not understand what we were trying to say. Language was a huge issue during the games and we weren't the first or the last Olympic athletes to find out the hard way.

So we decided to have a second crack at it. For the second time the bus completed a full circle with us in it. We could not even call anyone, as we had not had the time to pick up local sim cards at the airport. Now we were in a quandary. Finally our luck turned. At the next stop a couple of Indians got in. Both sir and I looked at each other and burst out laughing. The sight of those two men wearing the Indian tracksuit was the best sight we had seen in Rio since landing. Turned out they were part of the Indian hockey team's support staff. We explained our predicament to them, and after sharing a laugh together, we followed them to the building that housed the Indian contingent. The chef de mission, Rakesh Gupta, and his team had been waiting for us and immediately assigned us our rooms which were on the first floor. We were the first occupants of that flat as the others had not yet arrived. I was extremely happy to see that I had a single room for the moment as it meant I could sleep uninterrupted. We both decided to freshen up and head for dinner as we had not eaten a complete and solid meal in the last twenty-four hours. After that we returned, called home to say we had reached, and then crashed.

Considering the exertions, sir had decided that we would not train the following day. The body needed to recover after the ordeal it had been through and it was important that we adjusted to the surroundings. I took the opportunity to roam around the Village and experience first-hand the feeling of being an Olympian. Breakfast was fun; for a change sir did not stop me from eating whatever I wanted, and I stuffed my plate with all things that are usually taboo, including a bar of ice cream. My next ice cream would come on the night of

August 14, after my final. Walking around the Village I realised what a privilege it was to be part of the Olympic Village. There was single-minded dedication among the athletes who were there. Be it early in the morning or under the hot sun or even at night, there would always be people training and jogging around the Village. The gym was always overcrowded as everyone tried to stay in peak physical shape. It was pretty intimidating for me but inside that Village I realised what it meant to be an Olympian. Only the best in the world make it to an Olympics, the qualification standards are set high to weed out those who are not good enough. Good enough doesn't apply to the Olympics; you have to earn your place to be at the high altar of world sport.

After that first day, set aside to recuperate, we threw ourselves into the training. The practice venues were different from the ones I had trained at during the test event. Gradually I got used to the facilities and within a couple of days was confident enough to wander around the Village on my own. Sir was having none of it and he forbade me from going anywhere without him. Most of the Indian team had arrived by then and I got along very well with sprinter Srabani Nanda and a few others. The women's hockey team too was very friendly; they too were at the Olympics for the first time and all of us had something in common.

Everyone has a superstar moment at the Olympics, I had two. I was eating lunch one day after returning from the training and suddenly heard a lot of commotion. Both sir and I looked up to see what was going on and saw a lot of fellow Olympians taking out their cameras and clicking photos. My curiosity was aroused and I went wandering to find out what the fuss was all about. Turned out Usain Bolt had walked in to have lunch, sending the entire dining hall into a tizzy. I saw him standing in a queue to get his lunch and came rushing back to tell sir that the great Bolt was in the vicinity. There was no reaction from sir. He just smiled and went back to his meal. Then said, "They will all be clicking your photos after your competition." The same day I came across Rafael Nadal having dinner with his entourage. I used to watch Nadal's clips online during my down time and it felt surreal to see the man in flesh and blood enjoying a similar meal to what I was having not too far away. The Olympic Village that way is a great leveller, Karmakar and Nadal are just Olympians there. It's a different matter that outside that Village Nadal is a global icon. I felt a sort of natural bond with Nadal because of my psychologist who used to give me his example during our sessions. She used to get me to follow the same visualisation techniques that Nadal did and I rely on those even today. I am not the one to walk up and ask for a photo, I am very shy and prefer to keep to myself. I hardly have any photos from the Olympics; all my photos were clicked by sir on his mobile.

The gymnastics club had assembled and I ran into all of them either at the training venue or the dining hall. We had met at competitions over the years and while not friends, we were all familiar with each other. The vaulting world champion from Russia, Maria Pasaka, would always smile and say hello, so would Gabby Douglas, a two-time champion at the London Games. Even Simone Biles, the favourite for the vault gold, would stop and say hi when we crossed each other. We weren't at the same level as Bolt or Nadal but within this tight-knit community there was healthy respect for each other's achievements. My triumph at the test event had marked me out as a rival and one to watch out for.

As we counted down to our competition, another big decision had to be made. The qualification for the women's gymnastics competition was on August 7 and the opening ceremony was two days before it. I did not want to attend the opening ceremony, but sir was insistent that we attend. He reckoned this was a once in a lifetime opportunity that could never come again. Seeing his enthusiasm and knowing that he could not go if I backed out, I agreed. You could make out the excitement in the Village that morning as everyone rushed off to practice. For four years sportspersons wait for this moment, the ceremony that signals the start of the Olympic Games. If you break it down, any gymnast specialising in the vault has just two attempts with a thirty-second shot clock in which to perform. Some like Bolt have less than ten seconds in the 100m. It really is pretty intimidating if you come to think of it.

We had been informed by the chef de mission that we would assemble below the building at a certain time. It was the first time I had seen most of the contingent together at one place. Nanda and the hockey girls were going and we all got together to click photos. If there is one thing that defines the opening ceremony then it is photos and lots of them. Those like the men's hockey team, the shooters, and the tennis players who had matches on the opening day, and weren't going, too were down there to mingle and see us off. Abhinav Bindra was leading the contingent at the march past and there was a huge beeline for him when he arrived. He was and remains India's only individual Olympic champion and had declared that these were his last Olympic Games. I was too shy and intimidated though to walk up to him and ask for a photo. He was posing for photos with almost everyone that day and he would not have said no to me, but I did not have the courage. Another player who caused quite a flutter was Leander Paes. The tennis legend was competing in his seventh Olympics, a world record, and had a match scheduled the next morning. But he was there too and happily posed with everyone for photos.

Olympic opening ceremonies are very grand when you see them on TV, for us they are an absolute pain. I understand the symbolism and the pride that comes when you march behind the tri-colour but it takes a lot out of you. Remember the female athletes were all in sarees and most of us were wearing formal shoes. There was a long walk, first inside the Village and then at the Maracana, which hosted the ceremony. I thought the opening ceremony would be nearby; I got a rude shock when the bus ride took more than an hour. After reaching the venue we all were put in a holding area where we had to wait for our turn to enter the stadium. I was pretty hungry by then and since I was watching what I was eating, I had to make do with popcorn. So hungry was I that I snatched sir's popcorn as well. I also ended up meeting Abhinav Bindra as he came and sat next to us. I introduced myself and was extremely surprised to know that he knew all about me and had followed my progress since the 2014 Commonwealth Games. His physio Digpal Ranawat was with him and we chatted about some new equipment that Abhinav Bindra was going to launch in India after he retired. Ranawat told us that the machines would help me train and recover better and I promised to visit their centre after the Olympics. Eventually I ended up spending a lot of time on those machines after suffering an injury six months later.

I was not too impressed with the opening ceremony but it was a special moment when we walked in. Look at the footage closely and you will see me along with a few others in one of the front rows. Perhaps they decided to go height wise which meant me and a few other four-foot somethings were not too far behind Bindra. The badminton players Jwala Gutta and Ashwini Ponnappa were in the row behind me and all around me everyone was clicking selfies and photos even as the stadium itself was lit up by thousands of flashes from people using their cameras and phones in the stands. One of those people frantically clicking photos was none other than Nandi sir. After the march past he made his way to me and handed me his phone, asking me to click photos. I knew he was in a very happy mood as he never allowed anyone to touch his phone. But that night barriers were broken; Nandi sir was posing left right and centre with whomever he found. The good thing was that like him there were thousands of sportspersons from all over the world who were soaking in the moment and doing just that. I too ended up in a few photos courtesy Nandi sir.

By the time we returned to the Village, the ceremony hadn't actually ended, but I had developed blisters in my feet and couldn't stay up anymore. I walked back barefoot, and too tired to even eat dinner, both sir and I crashed immediately. Thankfully that popcorn kept me going, but poor sir definitely slept on an empty stomach.

Mercifully the blisters were not going to affect my training and we set out for an early breakfast. We were told to assemble, as Sachin Tendulkar was to visit the Indian contingent that day. Sir made it clear to the chef de mission that we had pre-event training and could not miss it. Thankfully he arrived just before we were about to leave and sparked off another massive photo session. I finally got my wish to meet the great cricketer and then left for the training venue.

My practice partners that day were Sweden's Emma Larsson, Slovakia's Barbora Mokosova, Vietnam's World Championships medallist Phan Thi Ha Thanh, who had pipped me to bronze at the 2014 Asiad, and Guatemala's Ana Gomez. All of us were mostly single competitors from our countries and were drawn together in a group of five for the next day. My first apparatus as part of the all-round routine the next day was the vault. I knew I had no chance of qualifying for the individual final of the other three and it was the vault or nothing. The practice went off well but the nervousness which my mother had warned me about returned as we entered the Village. I met PV Sindhu in the dining hall and she wished me the best for qualifying the next day. I got back to the room and with nothing to do, I went down and watched the action on the TV at the entrance to our building. I saw the men's gymnastics qualifying sessions as well as the men's hockey match where India survived a late fight back from Ireland.

I have the ability to forget everything else when I sleep; the tension sort of hits me when I wake up, so I slept well. The same however can't be said of sir. He barely slept two hours that night and the tension on his face was evident. He was on the edge that morning, the moment he saw me he kept telling me that I would start with the Produnova and then move on to the 720. We had decided that we would leave straight from breakfast so we carried our kit with us. Sir was insistent that I eat a very heavy breakfast, it would be roughly five hours before our subdivision got underway and he knew that I did poorly if I was hungry. There was no time to return back to the Village for lunch so we tucked in and left for the venue.

As luck would have it I was drawn in the same subdivision as Brazil. That meant that the whole attention was on them. Every Brazilian gymnast that day kept drawing massive cheers, which was good for me as it meant no one would be paying too much attention to a solitary gymnast from India. After the warm-ups I kept visualising my technique and the landing till it was time to go to the competition arena. The vault was my strongest suit and I wanted to cross the 15 point margin, which I felt was good enough to get me into the final. I was so wrong. When my turn came I thundered down the runway and got the Produnova spot on. The scoreboard flashed 15.100. Now all I had to do was deliver a second solid vault and I would be in the final. My landing though was low and I knew immediately that it would cost me points. How badly, I didn't know. I waited for the scores and then it came. 14.600, which took my average to 14.850. Decent but not good enough. I told sir I had messed it up. At that point I was sixth and knew that with other powerful gymnasts to come I was done. I still had to complete the other three events and did as best as I could. Sir was extremely happy when I completed my set. He said it didn't matter if I didn't qualify as I had given my best and was now an Olympian. As we walked out I saw a solitary man in the stands waving the Indian tricolour. It immediately lifted my spirits; at least someone was out there supporting me.

I wanted to head back to the Village, convinced that I had no chance. But sir was having none of it. He wanted to wait and see how the competition unfolded. I went, changed, and joined him in the stands. We were extremely hungry by then but sir was carrying neither money nor a credit card. He had not exchanged any dollars to the Brazilian real as there was no need at the Village, where everything was taken care of. All the vending machines inside the competition arena needed either a credit card or local currency and similar was the case with the food stalls. No one was exchanging the dollars and it didn't strike us to hunt for food in the athletes' lounge. So there we were—hungry, miserable, thirsty, and hopeful.

I knew that Simone Biles would qualify and when she did I got pushed down to seventh. By this time I felt that I would end up being a reserve just like the World Championships in 2014. Even sir felt that it was slipping away. There were still a few good gymnasts to come and conventional logic suggested I would be out of the race. It got too much for me and I started crying. Comfort came from an unexpected quarter. Gymnastics legend Svetlana Boginskaya was sitting a few seats away and she tried to lift my spirits. She herself was a three-time Olympic champion and had been my idol Oksana's teammate at the 1992 Olympics. Now she was part of Oksana's team and wore a Team Oksana T-shirt that day. She praised my performance and told me that I would make it. There was another judge sitting there as well, observing the competition, and she too lifted my spirits saying that I would go through.

As a gymnast you know who are your main challengers and I knew that the Canadian team had some strong vaulting specialists. If any of them got through then I would be down to eighth and a sitting duck. Even one freak performance could then end my Olympic dream. As expected Shallon Olsen landed two great vaults and took the sixth place. Her place was more or less assured while I was a nervous wreck. One main contender remained, Japan's Asuka Teramoto, who had been a gold medallist at last year's Asian Championships, though not in the vault. I knew that this was it, if she didn't do well then I was through. I looked at sir, he too knew what was going through my mind but he wasn't looking at me. Both his eyes were closed. My luck was in, Teramoto got a low landing on one of her vaults and even before the score flashed on the board below I knew I had made it. Boginskaya and the judge who was sitting besides us too got up to hug me and told me that I was through. They knew more about the sport than I did and knew the score that would come Teramoto's way. When it flashed we all were right. It was a 14.800 and that meant I stayed in eighth. The French team were still to finish, the last of the competition, but I knew that they were not capable of the high scores that would push me down from eighth. Sir didn't share my optimism; he as always erred on the side of caution and refused to accept my logic till the final results were declared. I was right, the competition ended with me on eighth place. Target achieved. It took time sinking in. I was in the final of the Olympic Games. A medal did not matter anymore; I had come to Rio to fight for my sport and country. I had done that by sealing a historic berth.

We finally left for the Village and reached at ten at night. I knew we both were extremely stupid to have waited so long. We had left the Village after breakfast and here we were returning more than twelve hours later without having had anything in that intervening period. We went straight to the dining hall where as it turned out social media had flashed my result to the rest of the Indian contingent. Rohan Bopanna was one of the first to come and congratulate me. The hockey team also saw me and stopped by to congratulate. Saina Nehwal and her coach Vimal Kumar made it a point to stop by and wish me as well. It felt as if I had won a medal, such was the euphoria among my teammates. When we got back we immediately connected to the Wi-Fi and I called home. Baba was overjoyed and told me that the house was full of well-wishers and members of the media who had come there for a reaction. There was no shortage of sweets from then on, ironic as I wasn't allowed to touch anything.

The next morning sir took my phone away. He wanted me to concentrate fully on the final. This even as he told me that we would take it easy that day and not train as we had been through the wringer the previous day. Breakfast that morning was special. Sania Mirza and her mother came and sat with us and asked about my competition. Seema Punia, the discus thrower, came up to me and asked me for my autograph! She said that the autograph would be priceless, as I would become a celebrity post the final on August 14. It was really special to hear all those comments. It showed that the contingent was in great spirits even though we had not won a single medal.

Without my phone I was cut off and did not know what was happening back home. Aruna though would call on sir's phone and tell me the exact nature of the hysteria that had gripped the country. She was also my harshest critic. After congratulating me she laid into me for not applying sufficient make-up during the qualifying process. She told me how my photo was splashed across the papers and how reporters were flying to Agartala to interview my parents.

Those photos though got me into a lot of trouble. They were all over and it emerged that I had committed a serious breach of protocol. Sir was summoned to the chef de mission's office and was told that I had worn the wrong costume during qualifying. Li Ning were the kit suppliers for the Indian contingent and had provided me with two costumes for the competition. They had come for measurements when I was in India and had asked for an existing costume, which I had provided. However one of the costumes, which had arrived just before my departure, was loose and I was not comfortable wearing it. Both sir and I were ignorant of the equipment rules and we had decided that I wear one of my old costumes which had the Shiv-Naresh logo! Someone noticed when the photos appeared in the papers the next morning and informed the IOA. It was a serious breach, completely unintentional though. The chef de mission was extremely supportive; he understood sir's explanation and dropped the matter by asking him to ensure that I wore the right costume on the day of the final.

My high had been punctured but not for too long. India's new IOC member Mrs Nita Ambani came to meet me and later that day Mr Srinivas dropped in too. He was extremely happy and said he had watched my qualification from the stands. He told sir not to put pressure on me as I had defied all expectations. A large credit was due to him as he had gone out of his way to support us in the months leading up to the Games, even bypassing red tape. He asked Nandi sir if there was anything else we needed. Sir looked at me and said, "We need Sajad."

In this entire euphoria everyone had forgotten the physio. He was supposed to fly out the day after us but he was still in Delhi, waiting for clearance. There had been some problem with regards to accreditation and Sajad was stuck. And with him so were we. So sure were we that he would leave the next day that we didn't even carry the usual equipment that we normally do. We had a bare minimum of tapes and Sajad was to carry the rest. Of course we never complained but by the time we had reached the qualification round we were out of tape. Sir had a basic knowledge of how to tape my ankles which used to swell because of the hard landings and that is how we managed. We were also helped by a physio from Mumbai who happened to be in Rio at that time and with whom sir had made an acquaintance at the competition venue. He went out of his way to tape me up the day of the qualification.

Srinivas immediately issued orders for Sajad's roadblocks to be cleared and tickets were issued overnight. The accreditation that he possessed was good enough for the training venue but not for the actual competition venue and he could not stay with us in the Village. But those were minor problems that were eventually overcome. Once again Mr Srinivas played a key role in my journey to Olympic glory. But as that story became known, it was given a completely different spin. I returned from dinner to find a spate of missed calls from Baba. He had been inundated with calls after a news item appeared which said that I had injured myself and as a result a physio was being flown in to Rio to get me fit for the final. Baba was at his wits end, my family was in a state of emotional turmoil, and the media was once again camped outside my house. When I finally called him back I could sense the irritation and concern in his voice. I assured him I was completely okay and that the physio's departure was to ensure I was in peak condition for the final.

The same evening sir agreed to let me speak to the media. There had been a lot of requests and since the final was some way off it was good to have it now than two days before the final. Unknown to anyone I had secretly been preparing for such an instance. There was no one to teach me or guide me but ever since my win at the test event, I had been looking at interviews of the likes of Sushil Kumar and PV Sindhu on YouTube. I taught myself to deliver answers with the same poise as they did and I must say I handled the interaction that night pretty well. Nandi sir wasn't too happy, though; I kept getting asked questions about the death vault and he was at pains to ensure no negative thoughts crept into my mind. The moment a question came he would jump in and say it is a very normal vault!

The next day was my birthday and sir was the first one to wish me when I woke up. There was no gift for me but he handed me his phone, as there were a lot of calls from back home. Thanks to Facebook everyone in the Indian contingent seemed to know that it was my birthday and everyone made it a point to wish me that morning. A cake also made an appearance but even though I cut it, sir did not allow me to have even a small bite. He went and distributed it at the IOA office in our building.

The next day Sajad arrived after a whirlwind trip that took him to Dubai, Sao Paolo, and finally Rio. And thus began our preparations for the big final on August 14. Sir was a hard taskmaster and now with Sajad there, the niggles were all taken care of. My rivals seemed to know more about me than I did. Steingruber, the Swiss gymnast, came up to me and told me that she had read that I was a celebrity back in India. I was pretty taken aback to hear that. Another gymnast from Romania wished me the best and told me to go for gold. She even showed me articles written by the Indian media. The internet has truly made boundaries vanish. All the other gymnasts used to come and ask me about the Produnova. They seemed pretty amazed to hear that I was not scared one bit. A lot of coaches came and exchanged notes with sir as well. In those seven days, we had become part of the gymnastics' elite. We were no longer the outsiders from India. But ultimately you are remembered for the medal. On August 14 I finished fourth, and returned to being an outsider.

THE HOMECOMING

Life has a funny habit of giving you a kick in the gut when you least expect it. After winning the test event in April, Aruna used to pull my leg a lot during training. She would keep telling me to up my game as I had to win the gold at the Olympics. "What gold, Aruna? I will not win the gold. But I may finish fourth like Milkha Singh and PT Usha," was my standard reply to her. On August 14, 2016, my prediction came true. I finished fourth at the Olympics.

Dealing with failure is an important part of the life of a sportsperson. Even the greats lose; it is how they rebound from defeat and win again which makes them truly great. That evening was a long one. Almost everyone seemed to empathise with me. I could sense the disappointment as well; India still did not have a medal at the Olympics.

There was a part of me that didn't move on. I was tired but could not sleep. I switched on my iPad and typed Dipa Karmakar on YouTube. I wanted to see my vault again, wanted to see if there was something I could have done better. You see one clip and then the next one catches your attention, it's a drug especially in that fragile state. My attention wandered for a while as a new clip started playing, it had nothing to do with the Olympics and I started to scroll over to a new clip when I suddenly stopped.

I recognised Ma's saree. Intrigued I started watching the clip and realised it was a nearly half an hour long clip of the celebrations at home in Agartala during my final. Baba, Ma, the rest of the family, they were all there, surrounded by media persons from all over India. Some I knew were from Tripura, having encountered them on many occasions. I was glued to the screen for the duration of the clip. The sadness immediately left me. It wasn't so bad. They were celebrating back home. Barring Ma and Baba I had not seen my family in close to four months and just seeing them improved my mood and I slipped into a deep sleep.

I woke the next day happy. It was August 15, our Independence Day. Sir and I went to the dining hall and I clicked a photo standing in front of the Indian flag. Nandi sir's prediction came true. Not just Indians, many sportspersons from other countries came up to me and asked me for photographs. I had never had this experience before. Usually it's the medallists who are feted, but my story had struck a chord with the rest of the community. It is as they say a great Olympic moment.

I was also very amused to read most of the things written about me. There were a whole lot of gymnastics experts who had sprung up in India overnight. Some attempts to ride piggyback on my performance had me really angry. It seemed that the Produnova was suggested to me by a senior gymnast. I was really upset when I read that. We had constantly been sniggered at, and treated as second class citizens at the camp over the years, and now the same lot were claiming credit. My journey to the cusp of an Olympic medal was all because of sir. There was no one else. It was his commitment and my determination. We both spoke quite a lot that morning. I was determined not to finish fourth again. I told sir we had to return with a big medal in Tokyo and if need be change our vault as well. The Produnova had served me well till now but it was a very difficult vault and even one small error saw points getting docked. Perhaps it was time to settle on an easier vault where higher marks would be awarded for a difficulty level lesser than that of the Produnova.

Sir reminded me that I had to sit for my MA exams when I returned and that it would be better to read up on my course work rather than get worked up over what I read online. I had asked Ma to get my books when she came to visit me and I had carried them to Rio. It is a different matter that I had not had the time to glance through them even once but now I was a free bird and had all the time in the world.

I realised I was fed up of being inside the Village. Every day since we had arrived we had either remained in the Village or gone off to the competition arena not too far away. We were leaving the next day and I wanted to go out. A few friends in the media took us both out to a mall where I enjoyed my meal of French fries and rice. I desperately craved for fish, and had already told Ma that the first thing I wanted when I returned home was some authentic Bengali fish. We returned back to the Village and sir decided to have a nap. I was more adventurous now. I went off to the competition venue to see the final events of the gymnastics schedule, the women's floor and the men's parallel bar and the horizontal bar. On the way back I stopped at the international zone at the Village and stood in line for nearly twenty minutes to get myself a nice big ice cream. I even got sir a burger and some fries and he got a pleasant surprise when I turned up at the apartment with all that food. Sir had some happy news to share. He had received a few calls from India saying I had been nominated for the Rajiv Gandhi Khel Ratna, India's highest sporting award. It felt surreal but I was not happy. I felt it would have been better had I won a medal and then won the Khel Ratna.

Later that evening Sakshi Malik won India its first medal of the Games in wrestling. It ended a barren period for India and you could see how that news spread like wildfire through the contingent. Sakshi's physio was my roommate so I waited for her to return with the complete lowdown. I had asked her to pass on my wishes to Sakshi and Vinesh Phogat the previous night. As I waited I logged on to the net to see Sakshi's medal winning bout and felt extremely happy seeing her on the podium with the Olympic medal around her neck. My roommate returned pretty late as she was tending to Vinesh who had suffered a very serious injury during the competition. Sakshi was nowhere to be seen as she had had gone to meet the media who had waited all this while for India's first medal. As I waited for her to return I packed and hoped to greet her in person. But I never met her.

Sir and I left the next morning for the airport with a tinge of regret. Time had flown and my first Olympics was over. I was returning empty-handed. I told sir that we would land in New Delhi and take a taxi to IG Stadium. I did not expect anyone there but Nandi sir interjected saying, "Pabla will be there." Fair to say, it had still not sunk in. After Sakshi's medal why would anyone care?

The trip back home was pretty eventful. We almost missed our flight. We were made to rush from one terminal to another and were finally told that our tickets had not been booked. Cue a few frantic calls to Pabla sir who assured us the tickets were booked. Nandi sir threw his hands up and sat down. I scanned through the tickets and realised the source of the confusion. Our first flight was from Rio to Sao Paolo and then a direct flight to Abu Dhabi before connecting to New Delhi. We had been presenting the Sao Paolo-Abu Dhabi ticket at the counter and that didn't show up without the first leg of the journey completed. We were guided to the domestic terminal and I ran towards it, telling sir to get the luggage. Thankfully we managed to check in on time.

A lot of people came up to me at the airport, especially Brazilians who had seen me compete and remembered my story. I was pretty taken aback to be honest but loved the attention. Most of them wanted to pose with me, attempting gymnastic poses, and it was all quite funny. We ran into Gagan Narang's physio as well and he came over and joined us. The flight attendants announced my name on the intercom when we boarded and a few Indian fans, who had come to watch the Olympics, came over to click photos with us.

There was a further reception in Sao Paolo with the Indian High Commission officers meeting us outside the airport and wishing us a safe return journey. As we crossed immigration I began to feel extremely low. I was headed home but I hoped for a miracle. I hoped I would get another chance on the vault, another attempt to get a higher score and return with a medal. Sportspersons are a selfish lot. They cling to that winning feeling. Perhaps I was more apprehensive over the reception I would receive. I told sir I didn't want to return home. I was not ready to accept criticism of my performance.

"Sir, let's stay in Abu Dhabi for a few days. I do not want to go to Tripura," I pleaded. I knew he would laugh it off but my nerves were shot.

There was some happy news waiting for us when we landed in Abu Dhabi. Pabla sir informed us that he would be there to receive us at the airport. He told us not just me but the whole of India will be there to receive you. Sir jokingly inquired if they were there to beat us. He also told us that Nandi sir's name was doing the rounds for the Dronacharya Award. Of course nothing was official and the meeting of the selection committee was a few days away but my performance and subsequent nomination for the Khel Ratna meant he was a front runner.

Now if that wasn't enough then imagine our surprise when we stepped off the aircraft at New Delhi. Standing right there, inside the aerobridge, were Pabla sir and our chief coach Bawa sir. I knew they would be at the airport but had no idea that Pabla sir would manage to come up right till the aircraft. It was a very happy and joyous reunion. Both of them garlanded us and lifted Nandi sir in the air. "You two do not know what you have accomplished," said Bawa sir. "Wait till you step outside," added Pabla sir.

Gradually we began to anticipate what was to follow. Everyone seemed to want a photo with me as we walked towards the immigration counters. There was another melee at the counters itself as the officers all came to meet me and requested photos. Nandi sir kept getting calls from the federation officials who were outside and Pabla sir informed us that we would have to use the VIP exit as there were too many people outside.

Too many people is something I can live with, what I didn't expect was the sheer pandemonium that broke out as we exited. It was late at night and we had hoped to catch a taxi and go off quietly to the stadium. Here there were at least fifty TV cameras, plus as many mics, and still cameras all thrust in my direction. It was pretty intimidating as in that melee no one respected each other's boundaries. Everyone was just screaming at the same time and I just could not make anything out. Add to that the never-ending stream of garlands that kept adding up. I felt suffocated and lost my cool when twice I was hit by the cameras jostling for an exclusive interview. You can speak only if there is some semblance of order, we realised there was no way that was happening so we decided to head off. A few familiar faces from the camp had also turned up and one of them, a doctor, had brought a container filled with the biggest rasogollas you could find. Before sir could say anything I had gobbled a few!

We thought we would get some sleep at the hostel but the media landed up there for their sound bytes. I felt bad for them and told them I would speak to everyone if they managed to sort it out between themselves and did not create a ruckus. That took a couple of hours and as it was already six thirty in the morning, we decided to head over to our gymnasium. Nandi sir, Bawa sir, Ms Kalpana Debnath, and I walked over and sat inside the safe sanctuary of my training arena, sipping tea and sharing stories. A lot of the trainees came over to click photos with me and this is where I actually enjoyed the attention. This was my space. We managed to sleep for a couple of hours after breakfast but then had to undergo a second round of TV interviews, this time live. Most of them had similar questions and I was pretty bored repeating myself again and again. While I was going live on television Nandi sir was busy answering the phones. I barely had the time; I spoke to Baba finally at nine that night. That evening there was another special celebration. The administrator, Ms Dayanand, organised a felicitation at the gymnasium and all the trainees showered flowers on me as I walked in. It was a heartfelt gesture and I was extremely happy.

The next day, August 21, saw sir being nominated for the Dronacharya Award. Finally, after years of toiling as a player and then as a coach, he would receive the coveted honour from the President. My promise to him a year ago had been fulfilled. Now we needed to go home. I had exams from 23rd and did not want to miss it. Once again Mr Srinivas came to our rescue. He told Pabla sir to send us home and tickets were immediately sourced. We were told at two in the afternoon that we had a flight at five, which prompted a mad scramble. On Pabla sir's advice we left most of our stuff behind at the hostel and rushed to the airport after a brief stopover at the SAI office to meet Mr Srinivas.

We had to spend the night in Kolkata, as there were no tickets from Delhi to Agartala at such short notice. It was all cloak and dagger stuff. Mr Srinivas had instructed the SAI officers in Kolkata that I was not to be disturbed and that no one should know of my presence. We were met at the airport by officials and taken to the centre. I am not sure if it was intended but I seemed to revisit my journey all over again—many years ago I had arrived at the Kolkata airport and gone to the centre for my first national camp. Mr Srinivas had instructed that I was to stay in the director general's room and not in the hostel so that we were not disturbed. The staff had prepared some lovely food for me, perhaps they knew I was craving a good Bengali meal and there was some excellent fish curry which was heavenly. Even Baba didn't know we were in Kolkata, he thought we would be flying in from New Delhi the next day and was very surprised when I told him I was in Kolkata. There was to be a procession from the airport the next morning in Agartala and the police needed my flight details to plan the convoy. Half an hour later almost everyone knew that we were in Kolkata. My teammates, Pranati Das, Pranati Nayak, and a few others who are based in Kolkata, called me after hearing the news and came over to meet us. It was great spending time with friends after a rather lonely twenty days in Rio.

As expected the flight to Agartala was an eventful one. Almost everyone recognised me at the airport and the inevitable selfies and photos kept going on non-stop. The Indigo staff sent the both of us ahead to the aircraft but this ensured a bigger problem. As the passengers entered the aircraft they saw us siting in the front row and everyone wanted a photo. Boarding took longer than usual to complete and the flight ended up getting late.

I knew Agartala would be a special welcome and I was not disappointed. We were ushered into the VIP room on arrival and that is where all the dignitaries met us. The authorities were not allowing anyone inside the terminal and even Baba was stopped. I had to send someone to get him and Soma madam in. Ma arrived later with the rest of the family and she too joined us inside. We were at the mercy of the police as the entire convoy had been planned by them. I was surprised not to see Puja around but Baba said she was at home as my niece Abu was unwell. Despite the massive crowd there was no chaos like the one in New Delhi. The police formed a cordon and I exited the airport building without being hit by the cameras this time. There had been a procession after my Commonwealth Games medal, this was grander. The convoy was split into three sections. At the head of it was a procession of bikes, followed by the open jeep where sir and I were seated. Then there were the cars carrying my family members and behind them were another twenty motorcycles. It seemed straight out of an election rally, only this time I wasn't watching from the road but was the centre of attention.

The police were stationed all along the route and I was amazed to see so many people turn out to wish me. Each time we crossed a school the jeep would slow down as I waved to all the children lined up on the roads on either side to catch a glimpse of the procession. It was magical. A bit ahead on the journey we came to an area which had three schools almost next to each other. They made a pretty sight, all in different uniforms cheering on someone who a few years earlier had been in their shoes, wearing a similar uniform. This was spontaneous, till the previous night no one knew when I was arriving.

Baba was in the jeep as well and I asked him if we could stop at my sister's house, which was on the way back. I wanted to see her and meet my little niece. Baba then let the cat out of the bag saying that Abu was in one of the cars behind us as she was unwell while Puja was waiting on the road ahead to surprise me. As we got there I spotted her standing on the road and asked the driver to stop. Before anyone could realise I had jumped out of the jeep and run into her arms to give her an almighty hug. I had missed her and even as the convoy came to a crashing halt I held her hand and dragged her into her house. The world could wait, our bond had been strengthened ever since I started going for camps and she was the closest person I could share everything with. As we sisters bonded, the entire convoy waited in the middle of the road. That my impromptu departure blocked the road was of little significance to me. Poor Nandi sir paid the price as he was admonished by a member of the force for not stopping me. When I finally returned I realised something was wrong as he was very quiet and looked red in the face.

A journey of fifteen minutes took more than two hours to reach the Vivekananda maidan, which is right opposite the Ujjayanta palace. The place was full, students packed the stands while people were gathered around a stage, which had been built in the middle of the ground. The jeep proceeded to do a lap of honour around the ground and I felt the love and the warmth of the people of my beloved hometown. As we finally reached the stage I realised that it was packed with dignitaries including our Chief Minister Manik Sarkar and other senior officials. All were on their feet and clapping as I made my way up along with my parents and Nandi sir. My extended family was sitting in an enclosed area right in front of the stage and it was a relief to finally see a lot of familiar faces. My friends were there too. I had told Baba to make sure they were around. I had made arrangements with my classmate Nomita didi to hand over her notes for the paper the next day to my family. We were felicitated, there were speeches and finally I was asked to speak. All the pent up anger that had been bottled up finally erupted. I had read some very uncharitable opinion pieces after my performance suggesting that I needed a foreign coach to take me to the podium next time. It was in very poor taste, especially as sir had been the man who dreamt of taking me to the global stage. After thanking everyone I unleashed my salvo. I reminded everyone that while foreign coaches were the flavour of the season, everyone seemed to have conveniently forgotten that the two Olympic medals at Rio came to sportspersons training under Indian coaches. Pointing at sir I forcefully made the point that behind my success too was an Indian coach. The crowd lapped it up and cheered. I even saw CM Sarkar clap very enthusiastically. Nandi sir kept smiling; he was intimidated in this company and in the presence of many of his superiors but I have always been a rebel. CM Sarkar was the last to speak. After the usual congratulations he asked the media to leave me alone as I had an exam the next day. He saved the best for the last. He announced my promotion as assistant director and Nandi sir to deputy director. It was completely out of the blue and both of us had a look of amazement on our faces!

It was time to head home after the function but I was told there would be a small ceremony at my school. I did not spend too much time there and after cutting a cake I said my goodbyes. My white T-shirt had turned black due to a mountain of garlands and I needed to rest after a hot and exhausting day. I had told Ma to prepare Hilsa for me and I was extremely hungry by the time I reached home. But the fish fry had to wait. TV sound bytes and exclusives do not bother about appeals by the chief minister. The entire media fraternity had turned up at our place. Everyone wanted their interview and after doing a few I excused myself. Sir came home after a while and took over the interview duties while I slept for a while. There was no respite in the evenings; the interview seekers had returned for the live broadcast. Everyone wanted a live show for five minutes only. No one followed the time frame and I started to walk out after five minutes so that I managed everyone's requests and also get the time to read up, which I did till two in the morning.

To celebrate my arrival the education ministry had announced a holiday for all the schools and colleges in the state. Everything was shut the next day. I happily accepted the exams getting postponed by a day!

The media followed me to the examination hall as well and that got me very irritated. I finally got to meet my friends but it was extremely brief. We made plans to meet after the exams as we were all in different rooms. I got into a huge fight with a few camera persons who had entered the examination hall, which was forbidden. I was not the only one giving the exams and the rest of the students were getting disturbed. That famous temper returned and sharp words were exchanged on both sides before better sense prevailed and they left and we could write in peace. The paper that day was Political Theory.

There was no end to the stream of visitors who kept dropping by—family, friends, Baba's colleagues, well-wishers, everyone. How I managed to pass those exams remains a huge mystery. The next day I got a phone call from Sachin Tendulkar asking me to come to Hyderabad for a felicitation ceremony on the 28th. You can't refuse him twice and I was keen to go as he mentioned that Sakshi and Sindhu would be felicitated as well. Now we were to be in Delhi for the National Sports Awards the same day and there was also a meeting scheduled with the Prime Minister on 28th evening. Once again it fell to Pabla sir to sort out the mess. He said he would coordinate everything and ensure that I would not have to miss any function.

All of us, Baba, Ma, Soma madam, sir, their son Akash, and I flew to New Delhi on 27th. After checking in at the Ashoka Hotel and spending a few hours, Baba and I left for the airport. We had a flight to Hyderabad at eight. At the airport I met Sakshi and her mother. It was the first time we were meeting since Rio and I wished her on her medal and we exchanged notes on how crazy our lives had been since we returned. She even clicked a selfie with me. I should ask her for a copy.

We checked into our hotel pretty late at night and had an early start the next morning. Thankfully the hotel was right opposite the Gopichand Academy where the felicitation was to be held. Aruna stayed not too far away and called me at night and I told her to reach at seven in the morning as I wanted to spend some time with her ahead of the function. As luck would have it she got caught in traffic as there was a marathon that morning and she reached just before I left for the function. I took her along as we were leaving straight to the airport from the academy.

We met Gopi sir; he showed us around the academy and performed a small puja as well for us. Sindhu arrived and it was quite a reunion as we all laughed, shared tales, and finally got to unwind out of the public gaze. I actually felt pretty jealous to see Sindhu and Sakshi dressed up for the occasion while I was in a simple T-shirt and jeans. Sindhu was wearing a lovely gown and I told Baba that he had to get me a similar one for Durga Puja. While I admired their style, they admired a locket I was wearing. Baba had wanted to gift me something when I returned home and I had told him I wanted a gold chain with 'For Rio' written on it. The proud father that he was, he had rushed off the same day and ordered it at a local jeweller in Agartala and presented it to me the next day. Both Sindhu and Sakshi were very impressed by it and told me they would get one made as well.

Sachin Tendulkar had arrived by then and he walked up to me first to congratulate me. He spent more than ten minutes with me and told me not to get carried away and to keep working hard, as this was the start of my journey. I introduced Baba to him and got him to click a photo. Baba is a huge Tendulkar fan and had told me on the flight that he wanted a photo with his favourite cricketer. Sachin Tendulkar had told me there was a surprise for me and it turned out to be a massive surprise as all three of us and Gopi sir were presented with BMW cars. He even clicked a selfie with all of us and I have never felt more proud. Later we met his wife Anjali who was also present there. "Oh, you are so small!" she exclaimed as she hugged me.

We were on strict timelines and headed for the airport the moment the function got over. I do not know who or how but a chartered aircraft was waiting to fly us to Delhi. There were seven of us on that flight—Sindhu and her mother, Sakshi and her mother, Gopi sir, and Baba and I. It was a memorable journey, some remarkable stories were shared and everyone was in extremely high spirits. All three of us had gone to our first Olympics, neither did they expect a medal at the first time of asking, neither did I expect to come fourth. Sakshi revealed she had barely slept a few hours since she had returned; I wasn't alone then, though none of them had to sit for exams amidst the felicitations. We were whisked off to Rashtrapati Bhawan as soon as we landed, as all hell was breaking loose. The rest of the awardees had already left for the dress rehearsal and soon we joined them as well. Sindhu and I had both received Arjuna Awards previously, but this was Sakshi's first trip to the Rashtrapati Bhawan for an award ceremony.

Later that evening we were taken to meet Prime Minister Narendra Modi at his residence. One by one we walked up to him to be introduced. When it was my turn he stopped me and asked me why was I walking and that he expected me to reach here by doing a somersault! It was a huge compliment and he shared his joy at our collective achievements. He mentioned how he had stayed up late at night to watch the Olympics and we returned from his residence feeling extremely happy.

My day wasn't over though. There was stuff still to be done. My luggage along with sir's had been left behind at the hostel at IG Stadium. So all of us crammed into a car, the three of us and the three Nandis. Soon after I realised I did not have formal shoes to wear the next day and so we all headed to the mall across the Yamuna which had been our favourite Sunday outing all these years, the V3S mall. I was recognised but Nandi sir was alert to get me out of there before I ended up posing for photos all through the remainder of the evening.

The Rajiv Gandhi Khel Ratna is the first award handed out by the President during the ceremony and is followed by the Dronacharya Awards and the Arjuna Awards. The three of us plus shooter Jitu Rai were proud recipients of the Khel Ratna. I was happy but I felt happier when sir walked up to the President of India to receive his award. It was an extremely proud moment for me; finally there was recognition for a man who had given his life to our sport. He had sacrificed everything to see me succeed at the top level. It was fitting that Soma madam and Akash were sitting in that hall to see him receive the highest award for a coach in India. They had similarly missed their husband and father for long periods. But that afternoon it was smiles all around. It was one of those rare occasions where the coach and his ward received awards at the same ceremony. I remember Guru Satpal receiving the Dronacharya Award in 2009 while Sushil Kumar was the Khel Ratna recipient and the next year when Gopi sir got the Dronacharya and Saina Nehwal the Khel Ratna. We had come a long way, the two of us. The Donkey and the Buffalo had survived the trial by fire. A new journey began that day, not one for recognition but one for redemption at Tokyo 2020.

Calling on the then Tripura Chief Minister Mr Manik Sarkar
after receiving the Khel Ratna.

The welcome party. Bawa sir and Pabla sir receive us
as we step off the plane from Rio.

The then SAI DG, Injeti Srinivas, meets us at the Village after my qualification. He cut through the red tape and ensured I trained on the best equipment ahead of the Olympics.

At times you do let your hair down at the Olympics.
Ginga, the mascot was adorable.

A first Olympic opening ceremony for both Dutee Chand and me. Everyone just kept clicking photos that evening in Rio outside our apartment block.

The Brazilian team were in my subdivision at the Rio Olympics. Thanks to them no one paid attention to the rest of us during the qualifying routine.

The legend PT Usha came fourth at the Olympics as well. To be even mentioned alongside her is an honour.

Need I say more? This is when Sachin Tendulkar praised sir for his dedication when he met us on the opening day of the Rio Olympics at the Village.

Mrs Nita Ambani, member of the International Olympic Committee, congratulates me at the Olympic Village after I qualified for the final.

Sania Mirza has been a pioneer for our generation. I was taken aback by her praise when she met me one morning at the Village in Rio.

Prime Minister Narendra Modi always makes it a point to meet the Indian contingent. He once told me he expected me to do a somersault as I walked up to greet him!

Small D meets the Big B! My fan girl moment at a function organised by NDTV in New Delhi. Grateful to the legend Amitabh Bachchan for his love and support.

A selfie to remember. The function in Hyderabad in 2016 was a rush-rush affair but no one complains when you get to meet Sachin Tendulkar.

A welcome like no other. Ma and Baba and Soma madam receive us at the Agartala airport on our return from Rio.

Humbled to have been honoured with the Padma Shri by President Pranab Mukherjee in 2017. My parents and Nandi sir accompanied me to the Rashtrapati Bhawan for the function in April 2017.

A proud moment for both families. My parents and Nandi sir's wife and son were there to see the both of us receive awards from the President in 2016.

EPILOGUE

Sport can be brutal, especially when you do not expect it.

The high of the Rio Olympics had not died down when my career suffered a huge jolt. A medal at the 2020 Tokyo Olympics was my target, especially after coming so close in Rio. But as I started my preparations for the 2017 season, I suffered a major injury that landed me on a hospital bed and not a podium as I had expected.

Getting over an Olympic Games takes time; winning or losing is irrelevant. If you win, then you celebrate but if you lose, then you suffer from what many call post Olympics depression. I did not win in Rio, but I seemed to be a part of almost every major felicitation programme organised by the government, states, private bodies, or societies. The euphoria lasted nearly six months but at no point did my training suffer. Back in Tripura, it was a 7 am start daily, and then another session to keep my body in shape in the evenings. The sport of gymnastics is such that there can be no long or extended breaks. Conditioning and control over diet is a must or else you begin the season unfit and way behind the rest of the gymnasts who are all competing with you for a spot on the national team. Sweets were a strict no-no even though there was no competition on the radar and the national camps too had not been scheduled. In between, I had to go to the office that I now shared with Nandi sir at the Tripura Sports Council in Agartala.

The national camp for 2017 began in February at my old training base at the Indira Gandhi Stadium in New Delhi. As the camp began, a niggling pain in my knees troubled me. Of course, after every session my physios would work on it and one sort of hoped that this was one of those niggles that would go away with time. At no point in one's career is an athlete completely pain free so you grin and bear it. One day though, it all came crashing down. I was on the floor, tying to do a 720 degree turn (the back lift straight body back somersault), which has a 0.3 difficulty score. This time I sensed that something was not right, the niggle had grown to an excruciating pain just as I started my routine. Before I could stop, the damage was done, it was instantaneous and the pain was too much to bear.

Scans revealed a tear of the Anterior Cruciate Ligament (ACL) in my right knee. Now those are pretty nasty and can be career threatening. You hear about a fellow sportsperson falling prey to that injury and you immediately have sympathy. When it happens to you, one tends to convince the mind that it is a small injury that will heal pretty quickly under proper supervision. I went to meet Dr Col BK Nayak in the Sports Injury Centre in Delhi at the Safdarjang Hospital and also took the advice of Dr Mrinal Dhawan in Delhi. Dr Anant Joshi in Mumbai who has operated on the likes of Sachin Tendulkar and other prominent sportspersons convinced me to undergo a surgery. Rio and the highs post it had disappeared as my career was now in jeopardy.

People often say that it is very difficult for a gymnast to make a successful comeback after an ACL tear. Now I understand what they actually mean. I am aware of the very fact that the pain during the rehabilitation process is very severe and that it becomes difficult for the sportsperson to cope with it, and ultimately the recovery becomes extremely difficult.

Throughout the history of sports in India or overseas, many great careers have ended early due to injuries. You just cannot do much when the body gives up or refuses to heal to a sufficient level to allow oneself to return to the levels that they were at earlier. It is a risk and that is why many sportspersons tend to avoid being operated on until no other option exists. But equally stirring are the stories of comebacks, as they tend to be remembered more and are spoken of in gushing terms. In Indian sport, there were a lot of headlines devoted to Sachin Tendulkar's return from a Tennis elbow many years ago. Yogeshwar Dutt came back from ACL to win an Olympic medal in 2012 and an Asiad gold two years later. At the time when I suffered my injury, world sport was writing odes to the longevity of Roger Federer who returned from an injury layoff in the second half of 2016, that saw him miss the Olympics and then win the Australian Open, the Indian Wells Masters, and the Miami Masters. These were the stories that Nandi sir kept repeating to me as I lay on a hospital bed in Mumbai. All costs were borne by the Sports Ministry through SAI and one cannot thank them enough for the effort they undertook to look after us.

One thing was clear, if I returned to the arena again, then the Produnova was out. I had to learn to compete from scratch, take small steps before I could even be close to the fitness levels required to be back at the national camp. Self-doubt eats you away when you are lonely but, thankfully, Nandi sir kept my morale up as I recovered. I sort of knew that the Commonwealth Games in the Gold Coast were likely to be too early for me. Mentally, you start telling yourself to accept the reality—that there would be no encore, no chance to win a gold at the Games. It is not easy. You want success. You crave recognition. Once you achieve it, then no one wants to see it slip away. Success comes at a great cost, in my case it came after a huge struggle. But somewhere you have to find a way to cope. I would watch my fellow gymnasts go through their routines when I returned to the camp. I was simply doing basic exercises, consisting of mainly a lot of rehabilitation and strength work. I had to build up strength in the knees. I would be doing the same routines in my head while watching the rest. One had to put on a brave face. They knew that I was hurting but one cannot show it. Sorry, no signs of weakness. Too much is at stake. The media cannot be told that there is no way I am headed to the Games. Optimism is the key. All the coaches, including sir, would tell me I was almost there. I was not even close. The months ticked by, December went by in a flash, by January I was attempting the floor routines but had not come close to attempting the Produnova even once on the foam pit. By the end of January 2018, there was no delaying the inevitable. The trials for the

Games were scheduled and there would be media around. The day before the trials it was announced that I was not fit to take part.

Before the Games came another warning sign that the sport had moved on and I had a lot of catching up to do. At the Melbourne World Cup, my friend and teammate Aruna Budda Reddy created history by winning a bronze medal in the vault. Rakesh Patra, Pranati Nayak, and Ashish Kumar also raised hopes of a good Commonwealth Games by putting in strong performances. But alas, the Games turned out to be a huge setback for the team. We had a few gymnasts reaching the finals but there was no medal, a hat trick missed for Indian gymnastics. It was painful to watch from in front of my TV screen back home in Agartala. The feeling of helplessness grew.

I was often asked as to whether I'd be able to make a comeback or not. I personally did not have an iota of doubt about it. Further, history is found to be full of examples where gymnasts have made a successful comeback. Aliya Mustafina of Russia is a good example of this. She was the star of the London Olympics in 2012. However, after an ACL tear injury, everyone started writing her off. But she made a phenomenal comeback and went on to lead the Russian contingent in all four events and bagged four medals at the London Olympics. Incidentally, she also won a gold, silver, and bronze at the Rio Olympics. Rebeca Andrade of Brazil ruptured her right ACL almost a year before Rio Olympics and was out of contention for her home Olympics for almost eight months. Rebeca is considered to be the strongest gymnast of Brazil and she made a comeback just in time for the Games. She performed well in the qualifications and helped her country qualify for the team finals in fifth place. Individually too, she qualified for the all-round final in third place. However, during the team finals, she accidently fell on the floor and her team finished fourth. The medal may not have been there but it is her return that motivates me. Incidentally, even two-time world gymnastics men's champion Diego Hypólito of Brazil made an impressive comeback after an ACL injury in Rio. Diego went on to win medals for his country.

There is no point rushing it. I cannot turn up one day and nail the perfect Produnova. The target is still Tokyo. Qualification will not be easy. But I have been hurting. I have never had as much time off from gymnastics since I started. Perhaps I will change my vaults, curb the aggression, and just focus on getting the basic ones first. The Produnova or something better can wait. A perfect Produnova in Tokyo in 2020 makes sense. Not now. The journey has begun once again. The Artistic Gymnastics World Challenge Cup in Mersin, Turkey, was my first international meet since the Olympics. Of course the doubts were there. You stay away from the sport for long and it all sort of flashes in front of you when you are about to compete. It had been three months since I started vaulting again. I had not tried the Produnova even once. I had been selected for the Asian Games but a domestic trial is no indicator of standard. The Turkey trip was an exposure trip at best and I was pleasantly surprised when I ended up winning it. My scores were not great but there is no substitute for that winning feeling. Mentally I was at peace. I was not finished as many were predicting. The Asian Games in Jakarta were again too early. I did not reach the final of the vault, with Pranati and Aruna getting higher scores than me. I did reach the final on the beam but was never in the hunt really and finished fifth. It hurt, it was another competition for the Indian team without a medal in 2018. Personally the loss of two years is a setback but I am back on my feet, I am determined again. Once again, it is the turn of the donkey and the buffalo to prove everyone wrong. We have done it once, and we can do it again.

ACKNOWLEDGEMENTS

Bishweshwar Nandi

I must confess I am a man of few words. I am pretty reserved and I must thank Vimal Mohan and Digvijay Singh Deo for pushing me all the way and getting me to open up on a very remarkable journey. Vimal has been one of my earliest backers and I admire Digvijay's ability to push the boundaries.

I never got much recognition when I was a competing gymnast. It did hurt me that I never received the Arjuna Award as well. But I have no regrets today. Dipa Karmakar has ensured that my name will forever be associated with her feats.

I am a firm believer in fate and I thank the almighty for setting Dipa and me together on what has been a fascinating journey. Many years ago it was Kamal Saha who sparked off this ride when he asked me to coach Dipa who was then training under my wife Soma. The future of gymnastics in Tripura was bleak then. I had seen the domination which was achieved under the late Dalip Singh but the conveyor belt had died up. Perhaps I too had accepted the status quo but Dipa changed that perception. She had stubbornness in her which would not allow her to accept defeat. For us, simple folks from Tripura, an Olympic and World Championships final was beyond our wildest dreams. Together though, Dipa and I achieved it and I hope this is the beginning of a new phase in Indian gymnastics. I was very inspired by Abhinav Bindra's gold medal at the 2008 Beijing Olympics and we are seeing how that one triumph changed the perception of Indian shooting and drew in a new generation to the sport. I sincerely hope that Dipa's performance at the Olympics has inspired many to take up our beautiful sport.

Dipa has been my most successful ward but I want to thank all those gymnasts who have trained under me from the time I began my coaching career. I have learnt along the way and their contribution cannot be ignored. Hopefully the lessons I have learnt coaching Dipa can be imparted to the new generation of gymnasts training under me.

One of the pitfalls of coaching is that you tend to get fully involved with your students. As a consequence there have been times when my family has had to soldier on, without a husband and a father. My wife Soma has handled my absence well and she remains a sounding board. Not once has she complained about the months I have stayed away from home and in camps. I am guilty of perhaps ignoring my son Akash, I have not spent as much time as I should have as he grew up and perhaps this is the best place for me to apologise to both of them. Had it not been for their unwavering support, I would not have been able to devote the time that I did in helping Dipa reach the top level in gymnastics.

It is extremely important to have scientific support when dealing with sportspersons and I am fortunate to have had in Agartala itself three doctors who have been of immense assistance to Dipa and the rest of the gymnasts training under me. Dr Juthsnamoy Datta and Dr Jiban Krishna Nag are orthopaedic doctors while Dr Saumen Chowdhary, a medicine specialist, has been a call away all these years. Sajad Ahmed Mir is no longer just Dipa's sports physiotherapist, he is part of our family. He is employed by the Government of Jammu & Kashmir but came back to our team to help Dipa's rehabilitation post her ACL injury in 2017. Sajad's journey to Rio can be the subject of an interesting book! Bhawna Chauhan, a sports psychologist with the SAI, has been working with Dipa from 2014 till today and she deserves a lot of credit for taking care of the mental aspect of elite athlete performance.

The Tripura Government offered me a job when I had none after my playing days ended and I must thank them for their continued support till today. Dipa's success has seen the state invest a lot of money in upgrading the facilities and I am confident that we will once again see a gymnastics boom in the state. To all my seniors, colleagues, coaches and well-wishers at the Tripura Sports Council, this journey would not have been possible without your support and encouragement. The Tripura Gymnastics Association have always backed me and I am grateful to the Gymnastics Federation of India for finding me worthy enough to be part of the national coaching set-up. The guidance of our chief coach, Dr GS Bawa, has ensured that I grow as a coach as well and I look back fondly on the time spent in national camps with him and the other coaches which has added to my knowledge of gymnastics.

I always read that sport in India is held-up by red tape but I have always had the best possible relationship with the Ministry of Youth Affairs and Sports, Government of India, and the Sports Authority of India. On more than one occasion, the SAI has gone out of its way to facilitate Dipa's training, at times clearing proposals running into lakhs within days. Former Director Generals Jiji Thomson and Injeti Srinivas who later served as Secretary, Sports, have been instrumental in backing Dipa and me all the way. I must also acknowledge Inderjeet Singh Pabla in particular for always lending a patient ear and ensuring that there were no roadblocks. Ms Manjushree Dayanand played a vital role as administrator of the Indira Gandhi Stadium leading up to the Rio Games and shielded us from the constant media attention that was focussed on us. It made her hugely unpopular but time was limited and we had to be completely focussed on our training. I will also commend the Go Sports Foundation for the excellent role they are playing behind the scenes.

Finally, to the Karmakar family. Both Soma and I have been blessed to have been Dipa's only coaches since the age of five. Over the years, the friendship with Dulal and Gauri Karmakar has grown and we are now part of the same family. There will not be too many parents who will blindly entrust their child to a coach and never interfere. It has been close to two decades now and not once have they ever questioned a single decision.

To the aspiring gymnasts reading this book. Dream, Aspire and Soar. Never take no for an answer. Always believe.

Digvijay Singh Deo

Patience is a virtue I do not possess in abundance. Thankfully, a circle of friends, mentors, and colleagues have constantly infused this necessary quality in me. Without their support I would not have developed the ability to be patient. Nor would this book have seen the light of day.

I realised very early that balancing a sports editor's role with that of an author was not just tricky but also extremely difficult. My fellow sports journalists will be well aware of this dilemma. Unlike other professions, we just cannot switch off when we return home. For there is some sport live on TV and despite one's best efforts to stay aloof, passion for sport ensures that another day goes by without a single line being added to the draft of the manuscript!

I owe a debt of gratitude to my old friend, Vimal Mohan, who agreed to be a partner on this remarkable journey. Over the years, Vimal and I have endured a tempestuous relationship due to our passion for sport. At times we agree but mostly we disagree. Yet, Vimal has been one of my most ardent backers through the years when I was coming up the ranks. We share a common passion to increase the coverage of Olympic sports on our respective channels.

Vimal was perhaps one of the first Indian journalists to back Dipa Karmakar and Bishweshwar Nandi. A regular at national camps (with or without his camera), Vimal had been predicting a great career for Dipa much before she won that breakthrough medal at the Commonwealth Games in Glasgow. To be honest, how many even covered a gymnastics camp before the 2010 Commonwealth Games?

Vimal is more impatient than I am, but through this journey he kept urging me to stay focussed and coaxed me to get over the line. If I may be permitted to draw a Tour de France analogy, he is the best wingman since Geraint Thomas.

My agent Kanishka Gupta has sadly been put through the wringer on this one. It was his infectious enthusiasm that convinced me to take up this project and all through the last two years, he has had my back. I owe him a great deal; it has been two projects together now and I can take a bit of credit for getting him keen on sports memoirs.

I also need to thank Shikha Sabharwal, Publishing Director at Fingerprint!, for showing great enthusiasm in sanctioning this book and then waiting to see it completed. We need more directors like her, who are willing to help tell the story of the Indian sportsperson. For almost each one of them battles adversity at many levels and makes it. It is never easy being an 'Olympic' event player in India. Thousands of such stories are waiting to be told.

Stuti Agarwal, for all her help with the various drafts of the manuscript and helping us clean it up before we could send it to the publisher.

I must admit I was extremely surprised by the simplicity of the Karmakars and the Nandis in Agartala. It says a lot about you that you can unhesitatingly open up to outsiders and let them into your private lives. Dipa's parents, Dulal babu and Gouri Karmakar, are wonderful and it is no surprise that their daughters, Puja and Dipa, are just as wonderful. The values the Karmakars have enshrined in their children is evident in the way Dipa conducts herself in public. You never get the feeling that you are spending time in a Khel

Ratna Award winner's company. There is such simplicity in her conversations and she says it straight from her heart. It is that remarkable innocence that I have tried to reflect in this story. I will never forget four of us—Dulal babu, Mrs Karmakar, Dipa, and I—cramming in the back of a Maruti 800 when we returned from Bishweshwar Nandi's niece's wedding in Agartala.

Both Mr Nandi and his wife, Soma, have been Dipa's rocks over the years. Indian sport will be in excellent shape if we have more such coaches around the country. The Nandis have never allowed the constraints of money or training equipment to shake their unwavering belief in their wards.

Most of us in the national media are swayed by the infrastructure we see in the metros. We saw rudimentary facilities in Agartala, which has produced so many gymnasts over the years, and now a superstar in Dipa. The complaint about lack of facilities is common in Indian sport and has always been offered as an excuse for subpar performances. Dipa's success and Nandi's dedication to help her get to the world stage destroys that excuse once and for all.

Many years ago, Leander Paes gave Indian sport belief at the Atlanta Olympic Games in 1998 and Abhinav Bindra destroyed the cynicism surrounding India's Olympic sportspersons in 2008. Dipa Karmakar shifted the goalposts for Indian sport in 2016.

Bharat Kishore Deb Burma, Mrs Sushila Devi, and Mr Mantu Debnath did not hesitate in welcoming me to their personal space. I am humbled by their warmth and hospitality. Sincere thanks are due to my college classmate Banoj Biplab Das, who assisted me in Agartala, and Gaurav Verma.

Amit Bose, my dear friend and co-author on *My Olympic Journey*, had told me back in 2016 that he would be available if I needed him. Amit and Siddharth Subramanian captured the wonderful pictures of Dipa training with Nandi. I am also grateful to Seshadri Sukumar for graciously sharing a few photos of Dipa competing during the 2016 Olympics. Sukumar's passion to shoot pictures is unparalleled and it is the energy of veterans such as he that motivates me to go that extra yard while on a shoot for a story. I must also thank Mr Satyajit Sankrit, administrator at the Indira Gandhi Stadium, for trusting us and allowing us access whenever we requested him.

Neha Rastogi is a friend first and then the founder of WordsWork Public Relations. She facilitated my request to connect with the great Nadia Comăneci. For me, gymnastics is still defined by Nadia, and I appreciate her time to write the foreword for this book.

I am thankful to Laureus for their assistance and to Gautam Seth for overseeing this in Monaco in 2017 at the Laureus World Sport Awards.

Shivani Naik, writer extraordinaire, of the *Indian Express* very kindly agreed to read a few chapters and offered her advice. My former Editor-in-Chief at CNN-IBN, Rajdeep Sardesai, remains a mentor, someone I turn to regularly for advice. He told me to go for it when I discussed the proposal after I returned from Rio de Janeiro.

I must thank the editorial team at World is One, WION, for their patience and understanding. Editor-in-Chief Sudhir Chaudhary has allowed me a lot of freedom to report on sport and never once has he said no to a request from me, however over the top or expensive it has been. I set up the sports team at WION from scratch and it has been a wonderful journey since January 2017. It also explains the delay in getting this book to print. I have a wonderful team which has backed me and I am thankful to Krishnan Iyer, Gandharv Jain, Yash Jha, and Rahul Dalal for holding fort whenever I have had to slip away for a day or two or turned up late to work.

One is blessed to have the company of friends who always offer a straight opinion and tell me on my face when I am wrong. Arunima, Manisha Malhotra, Neeru Bhatia, and Vinayak Padmadeo have always been there for me, be it with a compliment or a reprimand. Nayantara Pani, over in Bengaluru, has always been pushing me to do more and so has Gaurav Kalra. G Rajaraman has been someone who I have relied on for advice and much more. He once told me that we remain students of sport through our careers. I believe it more firmly now. Kamesh Srinivasan continues to be a sounding board for all things sport.

I have been reporting on sport since 2003 and have seen some really great champions stand by me. Ronjan Sodhi is a buddy, a constant support, and family. Manavjit Sandhu and Akhil Kumar have never said no to me. Thank you for being my pillars of support. Abhinav Bindra may have retired but our conversations on sport have not stopped and he continues to inspire me to aim higher.

Enrico Piperno, Pullela Gopichand, Anjali Bhagwat, Suma Shirur, Sushil Kumar, Vijender, Gagan Narang, Sania Mirza, Yogeshwar Dutt, Saina Nehwal, MC Mary Kom, Ashwini Ponnappa, Ronak Pandit, Heena Sidhu, and PR Sreejesh are a call or a WhatsApp message away. Perhaps, one day I will be allowed to write my own memoirs about the times spent with such wonderful people off camera.

Raninder Singh, president of the NRAI, has also been there in the good times and bad. We clash on shooting related matters but our shared passion for the sport ensures that our wonderful relationship is not affected one bit.

I am grateful to Sameer Manchanda, Bharatendu Kabi, Anirudh Chaudhry, Prashant Agarwal, Rajen Garabadu, Manoj Menon, Ankit Sawhney, Girish Nair, Santosh Barodia, Vijay Dubey, Rishi Sinha, and Surya Gangadharan for their support and assistance.

Finally, my wife Sudeshna has always backed every decision of mine, including the important one to move organisations when I was refused permission to write this book. From reading drafts to pushing me to stop being lazy, she has been constantly involved in this book.

Life is full of small ironies and, in early 2017, when I started to write the first draft, our son Vaivasvat came home from school and demanded that he be enrolled in gymnastics class after school. He has moved on to football and continues to be fascinated by sport. Of late, he sits with me and watches Liverpool FC play.

Hopefully this book inspires parents to allow their children to play sport.

Vimal Mohan

There should be no doubt that a book of this kind would not have been possible without the support and encouragement, guidance and prodding, of a number of people. I simply cannot thank each of these people enough for helping me finish this cherished and important assignment.

My Maa and Daddy never forced me to do anything but would always say, "Work hard and be honest." This sounds like typical middle-class philosophy but has always guided me in both professional as well as personal front. My wife Mouli and our lovely kids, Yagya and Krishanu, have been my support system and bore the brunt of my mood swings during this period while I chased deadlines. My parents, my brothers (Anand, Vijay, and Raj, and their lovely kids Kushagra and Priyanshu) and their families have always shared my joys and sorrows and it was no different during this emotional, tiring, yet very fulfilling journey. My brother-in-law Vishal would proofread my work, unmindful of when I mailed him a chapter or two. He and his family (Reena, Garv, and Trisha) never complained about him working at odd hours for my work. The enthusiasm of my mother-in-law and father-in-law, a sports freak, kept me focused.

I have to thank my ex-boss Sundeep Misra, who had immense faith in my ability and would always ask me to write books on Indian sports. He would often tell me that there is very little quality research done in this field and would push me to do the same. Mr KP Mohan and G Rajaraman are always my greatest critics and sources of inspiration. These seniors, in a way, always coaxed me to move forward and do something better for Indian sports. Mr Neeraj Jha, a journalist with Ten Sports, called me up during the Rio Olympic Games in 2016, endorsing my belief in Dipa's ability. A very dear friend from News18 India, Mr Vimal Kumar, was very keen that I write a book on Dipa Karmakar.

I recall the moment when I approached Mr BS Nandi with the idea of this book. Both Nandi sir and Dipa showed immense faith with their ready acceptance. Their faith in my commitment motivated me no end. My friend Mr Digvijay Singh Deo instantly agreed to share the responsibility of writing this book. I could not have asked for a better co-author.

Post Rio, I spoke to Mr Kanishka Gupta, a man of immense patience. Thanks to him, we secured a book deal in quick time. Ms Shikha Sabharwal, Publishing Director at Fingerprint!, has been very enthusiastic and kept us motivated throughout the process of writing this book.

I have spent more than fifteen years working with NDTV. I cannot think of completing this book without thanking Dr Prannoy Roy and Mrs Radhika Roy, two amazingly humble souls, for creating one of the best journalistic outfits. I thank my seniors in NDTV for granting me the permission to write this book. Mr Manoranjan Bharti, Mr Sunil Saini, Mr Aunindyo Chakravarty, and Ms Afshan Anjum were generous in granting me time off from work, as and when I required. Mr Sunil Saini and Mr Manoranjan Bharti would specially encourage me and give me enough creative space to do new things. Mr Ravish Kumar and I rarely get to interact with each other but he is a master news storyteller and I was moved when he wrote a rather flattering piece about my relationship with stars from Olympic sports. It came as massive encouragement while writing this book.

I have been blessed to have the rock-solid support of Ms Anasuya Mathur. She has always been a great support in all of my creative assignments. My colleagues Mr Deepak Choubey, Ms Aditi Rajput, Mr Rajnish Kumar, Mr Manhar, Mr Prafulla Kumar Mishra, Mihir Gautam, Shailendra Kumar Kanth, Mr Rupen Pahwa, Mr Ajay Sharma, and Mr Priyadarshan, Hridayesh Joshi, Madhusudan Srinivas, Ms Aditi Bhal, Bharat Bhushan, Santosh Kumar, Basant Jha, Saroj, Rajeev Ranjan, Sushil Bahuguna, Praveen Kumar Mishra, Navneet Kohli, Vandana Chopra and Devna Dwivedi have all been my pillars of support over the years.

My colleagues on the sports desk, Mr Sanjay Kishore, Mr Soumit Mohan, Jaideep Bhandarkar, Gaurika Chopra, Rica Roy, Mr Mahavir Rawat, Mr Shashank Singh, and Mr Sachin Srivastava were very supportive of this project. The have coaxed me to share my sporting experiences and sharpen the edges in different chapters of this book. I cannot forget how my erstwhile colleague Mr Kunal Wahi would constantly push me to write a book.

I cannot forget the show of faith that Mr Nikhil Naz had for me back in 2014 when I spoke glowingly about Dipa's chances of making an impact in the Olympic Games. He recalled my prognosis soon after her fourth-place finish in Rio in 2016.

I must also thank Ms Anjilee Istwal, who was responsible in setting me on my writing journey. She was the first to recommend my name to Room to Read and International Cricket Council, which offered me the chance to write my first book for underprivileged children, *Virat Ki Paari*.

Ms Richa Lakhera, an author, painter, journalist, and a very dear friend, suggested that we trace Dipa's history through photographs as well. So, we made a few more short trips to Tripura to get some original pictures. Our friend, Mr Amit Bose, was with us when we flew to Agartala to help with the visuals that you see in the book.

A group of talented youngsters who have joined NDTV were always ready to help with their research abilities and new ideas. To have these young friends like Pritish Bhatt, Gaurav Tamrakar, Amit Pandey, Sameeksha Sharma and others became a source of strength for me.

A number of my friends have helped in diverse ways. Mr Sudhir Kumar, who works in the State Bank of India and is always enthusiastic about sporting personalities, became a part of my support system for this project.

My schoolmates, Dr Kushal Chaudhary, Avinash Kumar, IAS, Harsha Jha, Manish Kumar Sinha, Niraj Singh, Amresh Kumar Sinha, Dr Dhananajay, Rajeev Upadhyay, Gesu, and Dr Kamini are the critical connoisseurs of my stories and articles.

While I was working in Sahara, a set of friends always had a different professional respect for me. Anubhuti Kaul Bhrany, Rajshri, Niraj ji, Deepika Bhan, Sweta Singh, Seema Singh et al became my guiding lights.

Some friends like Daya Shankar sir, my ex colleague at NDTV.com and BK Tripathi uncle kept encouraging me and believing in my zeal for quality. Some journalist friends like Abhishek Dubey, Mr B Vijaymurthy, Shailesh Chaturvedi, Pravin Sinha, and Norris Pritam sir have always treated my work with special respect and this in turn has helped me move tirelessly in this profession. To have friends like Mukesh

Anand, Shah Raza Mohammad, and Rajesh Kumar alias Chhotna is a privilege, as they have always given unconditional support in all walks of life.

Mr Pankaj Thakur, a senior IPS officer, was always there for us with his unconditional support. Anand Prakash, Avinash Alok, Keshav Chandra, IAS, Dr Piyush Ranjan, CRPF Commandant Rakesh Kumar, Acharya Kamal Deo, Sanjay Pandey, Chandrajit Poddar, Filmmaker Rakesh Kumar, super engineer Hare Krishna Verma, Mukul Kumar, Prasoon Mishra, Rajesh Jha, Rupesh Kumar, Sudhir Shyam, Vibhas Chandra Verma, Aditya Kant, Vijay Kumar Sinha, Solomon Yash Kumar Minz, Alok Ranjan, Amrendra Kumar, Kislay Kanth, and a senior Sanskrit scholar Saurabh Mishra always stood by me with their helping attitude.

Some of my schoolmates of Netarhat School, Om Prakash—an IPS officer in Rajasthan, Dr Gautam Sharan—an Oncologist, and an IRS official Abhishek Kumar, my seniors Rakesh Sinha, Member of Parliament, Rajya Sabha and Sanjay 93 sir were always ready to provide all kind of support to me. I must specially acknowledge the consistent support of Keshav Chandra who has been with me all through the ups and downs of life.

My senior in Netarhat School, Sudhanshu Shekhar Jha, who is a senior IRS officer and a filmmaker, seemed inspired by Dipa Karmakar's story and showed some interest in making a film on Dipa's life. It boosted us in our endeavour.

There have been several nights that I have spent in Col Dharmendra Kumar's home in the Delhi cantonment to be able to take early morning flights to Agartala. Each of my visits would have disturbed his family and their privacy but they accommodated me without hesitation. I am lucky to have the unflinching support of such friends.

My doctoral guide, Dr Bandana Pandey, was kind enough to give me time to finish this assignment. Dr MM Rehman of Delhi University was perhaps as enthusiastic about the book as I was. My mentor, Guru, and friend, Mr Jitendra Ramprakash, has always had more faith in me than I have in myself.

Mrs Anamika, English lecturer, and Mr Chetananand Singh, Executive Editor, Banking Services Chronicle, helped the narration get the right direction with their valuable inputs. They helped edit a few chapters and suggested some changes to broaden the audience beyond those who are inclined towards sport.

Having known Col Rajyavardhan Rathore from the days before he became the first individual silver medallist in the Olympic Games in 2004, I must say I have been fortunate to have many interactions with him, even after he became a Union minister. He has constantly been goading me to 'do something big'.

Sports Authority of India officials Mr Satyajit Sankrit, Mr IS Pabla, and Dr Manjushree Dayanand have extended a helping hand in the making of this book. Ms Shivani Naik of *The Indian Express* and Ms Sharda Ugra of ESPNcricinfo helped me draw outlines for some chapters. I knew I was on the right track when I found such support. Mr Harpal Bedi, Mr V Krishnaswamy, Mr G Rajaraman, and Mr Rakesh Rao from *The Hindu* kept pushing me to complete this project. Mr Prabir Das, *India Today's* stringer in Agartala, was of immense help with contacts and was our interpreter too.

The magnitude of this book grew because of the support of Mrs Sushila Devi (wife of the late coach Dalip Singh), her daughter Ms Sarda Singh, Tripura's first gymnast to win a gold medal in the National Championships, Mr Bharat Kishore Deb Burma and his family, Tripura's first gymnast to get the Arjuna Award, Mr Mantu Debnath, Ms Kalpana Debnath, Ms Banasree Debnath, and Dipa's friend, Ms Nomita. There are many whom I have not been able to name here but they have given me different perspectives about Dipa's story and I am deeply grateful to them all.

Last but not the least, a big round of thanks to Dipa Karmakar, her father Mr Dulal Karmakar and family, and BS Nandi sir and Soma madam.

I hope this book achieves its aim of inspiring the young to pursue their dreams by following the basic attributes of sincerity, dedication, and discipline. If this book is able to do that, Digvijay and I will have succeeded in our efforts to tell a wonderful story and add to the impact that humble Dipa has already made in India.

Bishweshwar Nandi is a recipient of the Dronacharya Award and is one of India's most iconic coaches. A five-time National individual champion, Bishweshwar captained the Indian Gymnastics team on six occasions, including the 1982 Asian Games in New Delhi.

A product of the famed assembly line of Tripura gymnasts created by the late Dalip Singh, Bishweshwar gave up lucrative job opportunities from government agencies to return to Tripura post his playing career. Since then he has been employed by the Government of Tripura and is posted at the Tripura Sports Council as deputy director.

Bishweshwar has been the man responsible for the emergence of Dipa Karmakar as one of the top gymnasts in the world. He has been guiding and honing her talent since she was ten. Together Bishweshwar and Dipa have redefined the goalposts for Indian gymnastics which culminated in Dipa's historic fourth-place finish in the women's vault at the 2016 Rio Olympics.

When not assigned to the Indian team as coach, Bishweshwar stays in Agartala with his wife Soma, who is also a gymnastics coach, and son Akash.

Digvijay Singh Deo is one of India's leading sports journalists and currently heads the sports team at Zee Media Corporation Limited's global news channel World is One, WION. He has previously worked with Star News, Doordarshan News, and CNN-IBN.

An alumnus of IIMC, New Delhi, Digvijay chose to cover India's Olympic sports persons very early on in his career and continues to strive to tell their stories, in victory or defeat or even in their formative years. In recognition of his contribution to the Olympic movement, he was chosen as a torchbearer for the Beijing Olympic Torch Relay in 2008 in New Delhi by the Indian Olympic Association. He has also served on the committee to select the 2015 Rajiv Gandhi Khel Ratna and Arjuna Awardees.

Digvijay has covered sport all over the planet and has interviewed global sports stars including Mark Spitz, Nadia Comăneci, Boris Becker, Roger Federer and Tiger Woods among others. He is also the author of *My Olympic Journey*, a book on fifty of India's leading Olympians.

From Odisha, Digvijay stays in Noida with his wife Sudeshna and son Vaivasvat Vijay.

Vimal Mohan is the winner of the prestigious Ramnath Goenka Award (2012), and has dedicated himself towards covering the Olympics, and any other adventure or marginalised sport, over the last two decades, infusing his journalism with infectious passion and unstinted commitment for the benefit of each sport and its followers.

He started his career assisting a famous media trainer, a documentary maker, and a poet, Jitendra Ramprakash, renowned film directors Prakash Jha and Ashwini Choudhary and subsequently moved into the Indian television space. Vimal's repertoire boasts of diversity, speaking of various films, documentaries, current affairs programs, election coverage, daily news programs, corporate films, articles in print and on websites and even a music video.

After brief stints at the Moving Pictures and Sahara News, Vimal joined NDTV in 2003, bringing with him vast experience in reporting and production, including memorable interviews with major sports personalities, all along staying true to his love for Olympic sports.

He has covered the Olympic Games in Athens in 2004, Beijing in 2008, London in 2012, and Rio in 2016, Asian Games in Doha in 2006 and Guangzhou in 2010, the Commonwealth Games in Delhi in 2010 and Glasgow in 2014. He has also covered 2003 ICC Cricket World Cup in South Africa, 2003 Champions Trophy hockey in Amstelveen, FIH World Cup hockey in Delhi in 2010, and FIH Junior World Cup Hockey in Lucknow in 2016.

Vimal was chosen to be part of the jury members of the most coveted National Dronacharya Award committee and Tenzing Norgay Award committee in 2018 and has also served as a jury member for the selection of Most Valuable player after the 2010 Guanzhou Asiad.